THE BIBLE

Its Heroes and Its Message

Marilyn Norquist

LIGUORI
PUBLICATIONS

One Liguori Drive
Liguori, Missouri 63057
(314) 464-2500

Imprimi Potest:
John F. Dowd, C.SS.R.
Provincial, St. Louis Province
Redemptorist Fathers

Imprimatur:
+ Edward J. O'Donnell
Vicar General, Archdiocese of St. Louis

ISBN 0-89243-227-6
Library of Congress Catalog Card Number: 84-52392

Scripture texts used in this work are taken from the NEW AMERICAN
BIBLE, copyright © 1970, by the Confraternity of Christian
Doctrine, Washington, D.C., and are used by permission of
copyright owner. All rights reserved.

Scripture texts — Proverbs 1:7, 16:18, 3:5,6 — found on page 91
are taken from the DOUAY-RHEIMS VERSION of the Bible.

Scripture texts — Proverbs 15:1, 27:14 — found on page 91 are
taken from the REVISED STANDARD VERSION of the Bible.

Contents

Introduction

Suggested Readings: Psalms 119:105, 160-167, 19:8-15;
Isaiah 55:10,11; 2 Timothy 3:16

Are Catholics familiar with the Bible? Most might reply, "No, but I'd like to be." Yet, most Catholics are more familiar with the Scriptures than they feel they are. Many of the readings we hear at Mass are readings we recognize. We've heard them before.

The difficulty we may have with Scripture is that we may hear it only at Mass. It is read to us in three small sections, taken from different parts of the Bible, and chosen according to themes. They sometimes have no other connections with each other. There are good reasons for reading Scripture this way at Mass. The reasons have to do with the purpose and balance of the liturgy and the liturgical year. The Church has selected the themes carefully for our growth.

Yet, we need to know how all these readings are connected in the Bible. We need to feel familiar with the Bible and to have a sense of its order. One way to do that is to learn about some of the Bible's events and people, in the order in which they appeared there. Each major event or person can be a kind of mental hook on which we can hang the Sunday Mass readings. Then we can begin to connect the readings and place them within the whole of Scripture. As we learn, there will be other — and wonderful — results, too. We will get to know and appreciate the Bible more. We will remember more and understand better. We will be able to make the Bible a larger part of our living.

This book aims to help you do that — to put the Bible in order and become more easily familiar with it. Each short chapter will discuss one of the important people or significant events in the Bible. By no means are all of the interesting ones covered! Roughly half of the chapters are about the Old Testament and the rest from the New Testament. These events and people are considered in the order of their occurrence, even though there is a lot of time between some of them. As the chapters flow, a clearer picture of the connections in Scripture will gradually emerge. The reader will gain a broad overall sketch of how the whole grand story fits together.

The book is designed to be a companion to the Bible, not a substitute for reading it! At the head of each chapter, reading suggestions are made. For this book to fulfill its purpose, it is important to read the Bible passages. In that way, your under-standing will be firsthand and much more alive than it can be if this book is read by itself.

The book begins with creation and moves on through the story of God's interaction with the Hebrews. The Hebrews were quite fascinatingly different from us; and that makes for our interest, but also sometimes for puzzles. Yet, they were also quite a bit like us, being human, so we can learn from their growing insights about God.

The first Bible readings, suggested above, will tell you what the biblical people themselves thought about the Holy Writings and what God said through a prophet about his Word. And please note: The Old Testament is as much the Word of God to us as is the New Testament.

The old Hebrews understood something beautiful about God's communication, which we have often forgotten. The Hebrews were aware that God is a mystery for us, that infinity cannot be probed by our little minds. Yet, they felt keenly his incomprehensible power. They knew they understood little of God and could predict little about his actions. They stood in awe of God, aware that if he withdrew his breath from their souls they would vanish. Yet, they also knew that they had to live in this world with or without understanding. So they felt a great need to know what God desired of them and whether he noticed them or cared for them.

Consequently, they cherished any communication from God. They could not know when he would speak to them or how or what he might say. They did know that to receive any communication from him was a privilege. Their experience was that God told them how to conform their lives to his good purposes. This relieved their ignorance. They praised God for his graciousness in revealing his laws to them. Even rules were welcomed with joy! With God's commandments available, they knew how to change the darkness in their lives, how to make daily life alight with God. Hadn't God himself told them how?

We begin, then, with the Old Testament, aware of our privilege and eager to hear what God said and to see what he did. It's also very interesting to see what the Hebrews did in response! As we learn, we can expect his light to shine more brightly into our lives, for the Word of God was sent through the Hebrews down the ages to us.

1. CREATION

Suggested Readings: Genesis 1:1—3:24

One of the most discussed stories in all of the Scriptures is the story of creation. It has been read and reread, argued and examined. It is very familiar to us — or is it? Do we really know what these three chapters of Genesis tell us? What basic realities about ourselves do they reveal?

First we note that there are three stories here: Genesis 1:1—2:4 is one creation story, written about 450 years before Christ. It climaxes several hundred years of Hebrew prayer and reflection. Chapter 2:4b-25 is a different creation story, written about 1,000 years before Christ. Its roots disappear into the most distant tradition of the Hebrews. Both stories talk about the relationship of God to his creation. Then chapter 3 is the story of the Fall of humankind away from its original harmony with God. All three chapters were written long before science existed, and we must not search them for scientific descriptions of how it all happened. These stories express inner realities that are more important than external facts: the origin of the universe in God and the two-sided nature of human beings.

The first creation story (Genesis 1:1—2:4) is a grand affirmation of the thorough goodness of everything in creation. When there was nothing but God, God created all the universe and its inhabitants. With every creative act, God sees that his creation is good. How could it be otherwise? God himself is perfect; his creation, too, must be very good. Genesis 1 rejoices in that goodness. You are invited also to praise God for the goodness of his works. (If you'd like to praise him with a psalm, try Psalms 136:1-9.)

The first story also tells us about the creation of humans. It says we are made in the image of God himself (1:27). That is not said about any other part of creation. Then God blesses the humans, gives them the "top spot" on earth. Gently, he provides them with necessary food. When God reviews it all, it is *very* good (1:31).

The second creation story (2:4b-25) pictures a perfect harmony between God and all his creatures. The garden is a paradise, and the human being is settled there to care for it. Everything God has created is brought to the human for him to name, thus effecting a relationship of knowing and caring between him and all other creatures. Along with the creation of woman, we are told that humans are free to live as they like, so long as they do not seek those abilities which belong only to God: life itself and the power to discern between good and evil.

Yet, these forbidden fruits were precisely those desired by Adam and Eve: " . . . the tree was good for food, pleasing to the eyes, and desirable for gaining wisdom" (3:6). Chapter 3 tells how they disobeyed God, tried to be self-sufficient, and disrupted the harmony which God had given to their lives. They separated themselves from God, and that separation is sin at its root. Sin also separated them from each other, as symbolized by their need for clothing, to be hidden from each other.

Interestingly, God did not remove the knowledge of good and evil which they had stolen in their pride. (He did prevent them, later, from gaining power over life itself.) But there were consequences. The necessary functions of humans — reproduction and work — were filled with struggle and pain; and eventual death was to come — "you are dirt, and to dirt you shall return" (3:14-19).

These consequences are still with us, showing the reality in the stories. Two things are always true about people: we are created in God's image and in essence are good; yet, in pride we seek power and knowledge apart from God (as if we could have anything at all strictly on our own!).

We see and experience both of these truths every day. People are wonderful — kindly and caring, generous, seeking to live harmoniously with God and other people. Yet, even the best of us is tainted by prideful separation from God, by that subtle desire to be entirely independent of him — at least sometimes. These Genesis stories are really, then, descriptions of our everyday life!

We will always know struggle and pain, and each of us will die. But we also long to be fully who we were created to be. So we reach out and try to grow. Sometimes we reach for something less than God, but only God will ever satisfy our half-forgotten yearnings to be in perfect harmony with him.

Growth is hard because the Fall is real. But growth is possible because the image of God in us is real. His image alone is eternal, and so we have full hope. Let us keep striving to get beyond the Fall, to reach again to God in obedience and humility. Only there is peace; only there is the paradise God created us to enjoy.

2. ABRAHAM

Abraham's Story

In full: Genesis 12:1—25:10
In brief: Genesis 12:1-10, 15:1-6, 17:1-27, 12:1-13, 22:1-18

When Saint Paul needed an example of faith for his new Christians, he could have chosen any one from many in his rich Old Testament tradition. But Saint Paul looked back nearly 2,000 years to the man known as the first ancestor of all loyal Hebrews: Abraham. He was the best choice, for Abraham lived an extraordinarily trustful and obedient life. (If you'd like to see Saint Paul's comments, look at Romans 4:1-25 and Galatians 3:6-9.)

Imagine yourself in Abraham's position: you are seventy-five years old, living in a well-run city; you have a wife and a large household of servants and relatives, but no children. Then God directs you to leave home and become a nomad in a foreign land called Canaan (later Palestine). What would you do? Abraham went! And all along his journeys, at important campsites, he worshiped the Lord at altars he built. The Lord stayed with him in a special way.

Abraham heard promises as well as directions from God: he would be the father of countless descendants; they would become a great nation and inherit the land of Canaan. Most happily, all the nations of the earth would be blessed through him. What an astounding expectation! But, as Abraham had no children, he had no idea how all this would happen. Nevertheless, he obeyed God. It was not all easy, either. His way was marked by problems, dangers, quarrels, and battles. But God was with him.

Years later God renewed his promise of many descendants through Abraham's wife Sarah: though they still had no children, one day their family would be as many as the stars! Abraham believed God. His faith opened the way for an extraordinary experience of covenant-making between the Lord and his trusting servant. It was a spectacular ritual communication, with sacrifices and darkness and the divine appearance in smoke and fire. It was surely an unforgettable moment for Abraham, a permanent and utterly sacred covenant agreement. (See Genesis 15:1-20.)

Even so, his future required still more trust. God told him that he — at ninety-nine! — and his ninety-year-old, barren wife Sarah would have a son who would bear God's promises. Abraham couldn't help it — he laughed! So did Sarah (Genesis 17:15-19). But he obeyed God's instructions just the same. Obeying, he waited. Indeed, Sarah did have a son; and they named him Isaac.

Was that enough trust to ask of one man? Apparently not, for when Isaac was a boy God pushed Abraham's trust to its limit. He asked him to sacrifice Isaac. Now Isaac was not only the precious child of Abraham's old age but also the focus of all God's promises. Everything that mattered to Abraham seemed endangered by God's latest inspiration. But Abraham recognized that his life was not built on his son but on his own persistent obedience to the God who had called him out of Haran years before. So once again he obeyed, not because he understood, but because he trusted God.

He prepared to sacrifice his son and was not stopped by the divine messenger until the knife was at Isaac's throat (Genesis 22:1-12). Today we often question why God would ask such a seemingly barbaric thing, or why Abraham would be ready to kill his own son. But our questions are based on our Christian understanding of morality, developed through centuries of salvation history. We must not read into the Scripture passages moral issues that were not intended in the original story. The only point here is that Abraham was ready to go to any extreme to obey God trustingly. His devotion to the Almighty was complete. Perhaps God wanted to found the Hebrew people only on an absolutely solid, human faithfulness and obedience. In Abraham God had that foundation. We ourselves can be grateful for Abraham because our own understanding of God came through his descendants, the Hebrews: the commandments, the prophets, Scripture itself, and finally, of course, Jesus Christ, born a Hebrew (or a Jew as they were called by his time).

In the life of Abraham we find many insights, but supreme among them is this: he went where God sent him and he did as God asked, always and trustfully. He asked questions sometimes and sometimes interceded with God, and he did a few dumb things too. But he was faithfully obedient. That enabled God's blessings to come through Abraham across 4,000 years even to us today. We have much to thank him for.

We may never be called to be as heroic in faith as Abraham was. In our hearts most of us probably hope we won't be! But we are asked to obey whatever we do understand of God's will. That often means risking ourselves with uncertain results. If we keep Abraham firmly in mind, however, we will remember that he found God trustworthy; so he obeyed him without knowing what the results would be. Just as God's promises were fulfilled through that obedience, so we see that, as we trust and obey God, the results in his hands can only be goodness. Like Abraham, we can count on God.

3. JOSEPH

Joseph's Story _____

    In full: Genesis 37:1—47:12 *(omit chapter 38)*
    In brief: Genesis 37, 39, 40, 41

_____

Our next story is about a person who began as a rather ordinary human being — a spoiled and arrogant child, in fact! He had no glorious encounters with God and no particular truth was revealed to him. Yet, he knew the secret of becoming a full human being so that his purpose in God's will could be fulfilled. That person is Abraham's great-grandson, Joseph.

Joseph's story itself belongs to a different group of stories than those of Abraham or Jacob. Joseph may well have been a hero to that ancient group of scholars known to us as the Wisdom School. They were men who observed ordinary life and tried to discover how ordinary people can grow and fulfill their lives. Joseph knew how. Further, God's action in Joseph's life was mostly indirect, as it often seems to be in our own. So, besides being a *very* good story, Joseph has something to show us.

Joseph was the favorite son of Jacob, who didn't treat his twelve sons equally. Naturally, like any spoiled child, Joseph flaunted his position. His older brothers finally reached the end of their endurance and almost killed him. At the last minute they sold him instead to a caravan crossing their territory on its way to Egypt. Nothing is said about Joseph's own feelings, but his separation from the familiar is a common experience of biblical people.

We need to notice that, ponder it. In the Bible, unfamiliar circumstances and the wrenching experiences that go with them are often the first step in a magnificent growth process. The familiar, comfortable parts of our lives seldom challenge us. Especially spiritually, it is usually necessary to be yanked into a new situation before we can give serious attention to God. But it need not frighten us because, even though our feelings are in disarray, we are closer to God than before. Genesis 39:2 tells us that the Lord was with Joseph. And Joseph must have cooperated with him.

Today we know that the Lord is always with us. Do we always cooperate with him in *everything* we do? Growing toward God means we must cooperate with him, even in the unfamiliar.

But Joseph's difficulties were only beginning. Soon he was noticed by the wife of Potiphar, his Egyptian master; and she tried to seduce him (chapter 39). Joseph refused to violate his master's trust so flagrantly. So the lady framed him — and sure enough, he was jailed.

Few of us have to face such a violent challenge to our faithfulness to God. But lesser challenges are often just as hard to handle, especially if suffering will result from our integrity. Joseph's example assures us that it is better to suffer injustice if necessary than to betray our integrity before God.

And the results are wonderful. The Lord stayed with Joseph; and very quickly he was in charge of the jail, and the jailer had no more worries! (Genesis 39:21-23)

We see here that God acts in ways we might not prefer. Surely, Joseph would rather have been freed, as we would want to be. But the Lord allowed Joseph to remain in jail for more than two years. Joseph grew. Like him, we can bear suffering with patience. We can do well whatever comes to hand. When we do, better opportunities will open up to us within the will of God. But God's timing is rarely like our own! If Joseph had been freed immediately, he would never have met the members of Pharaoh's household (Genesis 40:1-4). Pharaoh was the very person Joseph had to know in order to fill God's purposes. Meanwhile, Joseph remained faithful to the Lord as he always had, and circumstances happened just as the Lord intended. If we remain faithful, likewise unexpected circumstances will bring to us exactly what God wants.

In the end, Joseph was the ruler of all Egypt, second only to Pharaoh. How it all happened you may read for yourself. His abilities had grown in the years of running the jail and overseeing Potiphar's household. Joseph used these opportunities — neither of which he had chosen — to give excellent service to his masters as to the Lord. So, when the grand opportunity came, Joseph was ready.

In our spiritual growth, we may experience stages much like those in Joseph's life. When we begin to take our prayer life seriously, we often find ourselves in unfamiliar territory. That can be very unsettling. But if, like the young Joseph, we remain faithful to God in prayer, we are led further.

The next step may be suffering. It could come in any form; but suffering along the spiritual path will always be intended by God to help us, to ready us for deeper relationship with him. We can choose to wait patiently, certain that God is active even if we cannot see far ahead. We can follow wherever God leads and be confident, for in the life of prayer there are many twists and turns.

In the end, we may not be given authority over anyone else. But if we persevere, we will be given ourselves — our true selves made in God's image, for we are only fully human when we fully follow God. The fulfillment of the image of God in us is *everything*. It is worth any suffering, any challenge, any effort. The Lord will remain with us all the way.

4. MOSES

In full: Exodus 1:1—4:23 (*Plagues* 5:1—12:36, *Wanderings* 12:37—18:27, *Covenant* 19, 20, 24, 32, 34:27-35)
In brief: Exodus 1:1—4:23, 11:31—12:51, 13:17—14:31, 16:1-15, 17:1-7, 19:1—20:23, 24:1-8, 34:35

When you hear the name "Moses," what do you think of? a wall of water? Ten Commandments on two stone tablets? plagues and miracles? Of all our images of Moses, the most important one in the Bible is rarely familiar. Exodus 34 says the very skin of Moses' face was brightly radiant because he was so close to the Lord. Moses was an intimate friend of God. That is how he became the greatest of all God's messengers in Old Testament times. He was the "founder" of the Hebrew people, since he brought from God the self-understanding and the laws by which Hebrews were to live and to worship. He had been called by God to do that; and after his first reluctance, he was completely given over to God in obedience. It was said that Moses was the meekest of all men before God.

Moses became the greatest hero in all Hebrew history because he led the people out of Egyptian bondage into the learning place of wilderness around Sinai. Throughout this saga, Moses is both follower of God and leader of the Hebrews. He brings to them what God directs him to do. He mediates God's will to them. Through Moses, out there in the wilderness, the most significant event in all Old Testament history took place: God made a covenant with Moses' people. It changed their way of life, their sense of identity, and their history. Thereafter, they were the Lord's own people.

Why did it happen in the wilderness? Why couldn't God have acted in Egypt — or 500 years earlier with Jacob in Canaan? Surely, God could have — but would the people have been ready?

Wilderness has special qualities that help people come to God. That is true whether it's a literal wilderness, like a desert, or an inner wilderness, like suffering can be. Wilderness is always a little barren and uncomfortable and insecure. We humans think and act differently there. Our habits and preferences are interrupted. We become aware of our neediness. We reach out more easily for help. We may also, like the Hebrews, complain and agonize. Wilderness opens to us. If we don't get mired in self-pity, we become more sensitive to our own inner life and to those around us. We learn that we must pay attention to life in order to keep it. Most important, we turn to God because we become acutely aware, as we wander in wilderness, that we cannot handle life by ourselves. We need God.

God takes people into wilderness specifically to bring us to that awareness. He wants to make us his own and to make us beautiful, individually and as a people. If we do not desire that enough or if we are insensitive to his will or put obstacles in his way, God may lead us into wilderness. There, he can bring us into covenant with himself.

The idea of covenant is part of our heritage of faith. A covenant is a solemn, ritualized, and most sacred agreement. In the Bible, covenants of many kinds are made; but the most common is between unequal parties, especially between God and people. God himself needs no covenant, no promises, no law. So, when he offers a covenant it is an act of pure graciousness toward people. In the Mosaic covenant, God instructed his people how to live so they could be prosperous and safe. It was his gift of knowledge so they did not have to live in ignorance of the truly good life. He guaranteed them results if they chose to live according to his covenant (we call it the Ten Commandments), and he also warned them of consequences if they ignored it. He was acting like a father, tenderly training his child in the best way of living.

The people were able to accept the covenant because the wilderness had taught them that they needed the Lord. He could and did rescue them from danger and keep them alive. Their acceptance of God's covenantal way of life was their manifesto of dependence on God. So it can be for us also. Instead of resisting unfamiliarity and discomfort and the sense of our own littleness, we can welcome them and let them open us to God. Do we need anything as much as we need him?

The Ten Commandments have long been used to examine one's conscience. You may want to do that still. But now, don't think of the covenant laws as rules you *have* to follow. Think of them, instead, as the gifts of a gracious God, which outline a wonderful life. God wants you to have the very best life and offers this covenant as a guide. The Ten Commandments express God's fatherly love for us, so we can know how to find peace and prosperity.

Almost all of us pray for peace in the world. Are we ready to create peace in our own hearts? If so, we are ready to live fully by the covenant-commandments given by God through Moses out there in the Sinai wilderness.

5. GIDEON

Gideon's Story: Judges 6:1—7:22

It's a wonderful story, well-told. It appeals to our imagination and makes us smile — Gideon seems to be rather like us! Yet, he does remarkable things for the Lord.

Between Moses and Gideon about 200 years passed. The Hebrew people entered the Promised Land of Canaan (or Palestine) and left their nomadic way of life to become farmers and townspeople. In that change they met the first challenge to their covenant experience in the wilderness. There, they had thought the Lord to be a kind of nomadic God, who understood about battles and finding water. But their concept of God needed to grow when they lived in farming country, where fertility was more important than water holes. They turned to their new neighbors' "fertility gods," who were believed to bring rain and to fertilize animals and land. So they often forgot the Lord. The Book of Judges tells us that they got into serious trouble when that happened.

The Israelites had no stable government at first, only the covenant law. When trouble came and they cried again to the Lord, he sent someone to rescue them from their enemies and to restore peace. That person was called a "judge," and he (or she, for women were also sent) kept a certain governing power after the crisis. It was almost direct rule by the Lord.

In Gideon's time Israel was troubled by nomads called Midianites. Even their food supply was threatened by Midianite raiders. So, Gideon hid his harvest by threshing his grain in a winepress where it would be hard to see. Now, Gideon was a nobody (Judges 6:15). That was exactly why the Lord called him.

That way no one could get confused about who actually rescued Israel from Midian. God wanted his people to understand yet again that *he* was their rescuer, so they would know him better and love him.

When the messenger of the Lord came, Gideon resisted. He knew he wasn't anybody the Lord could use, and he was uncertain about this call: did it really come from the Lord? And would the Lord really do what he said he would? So Gideon needed lots of reassurance. First he begged the messenger not to go away while he prepared food. The messenger waited — it must have taken hours — and turned the offered food into sacrifice by a miracle of fire, then disappeared. That was enough to prompt Gideon's first act of obedience: to tear down the village symbol of their fertility god, a pole, so it would be clear that all following events were not the work of that god.

But Gideon needed more reassurance from the Lord for his next tasks. He put out a fleece and asked for it to be made wet and the ground left dry. So it happened. Then he wanted it reversed — dry fleece and wet ground. That, too, happened. So Gideon believed the Lord and obeyed the rest of his instructions, which included using only 300 fighting men in an imaginative and successful "attack" on the large Midianite camp. The Lord had already sent some 31,000 soldiers home!

Again, the Lord worked through human weakness so that his saving action might be clearly recognized. Why is that important? Because God seeks *our* good. God created us for union with him. Nothing less will fulfill us. The whole Bible tells how God tries over and over to convince us of that without turning us into choiceless robots. It is all for *us*. When great things happen through weak people, they show us what God is really like and what we are really like. We can't do anything significant with our own strength. We are not strong in ourselves! But we often deceive ourselves and *feel* we are strong enough without God.

God, then, may choose other weak people, or even our own weaknesses, to show clearly how mistaken we are. When we see our error and experience God's loving power we move closer to him. *That* is most important for us, and it is God's own desire as well.

Now, what about that fleece? Wasn't that "tempting God"? No, for Gideon's heart was sincere and honest. He was not arrogantly demanding proof of God, saying "I don't believe you — prove yourself to me!" That is tempting God. Gideon, in honesty and humility, was saying, "Lord, you've asked me to do a big thing, and I doubt *myself* very much. I need reassurance that you are really with me. Help me in this weakness." That kind of sincerity, based on a willingness to obey, always calls forth from God a clear answer.

Many of us have never felt specially called by God. We know from the Bible that God calls those who are fit for his purposes. Are we fit to be used? Gideon knew he was nothing at all. Do we know that deep within ourselves? Are we as sincere as Gideon? Our sincerity is more valuable than any talent we have.

You may want to ponder Jesus' meaning when, some 1,100 years after Gideon, he said, "Apart from me you can do nothing." (See John 15:4-8.) Reflect on this, and ask God to give you insight. Then you may want to pray with the psalmist, praising God, for

... the kindness of the LORD is from eternity
to eternity toward those who fear him (Psalm 103).

6. DAVID

From his youth, when he killed a bear, a lion, and Goliath the giant, David did everything in a big way. His dedication to God was wholehearted and determined. His passion to be king was no less determined. His talents were huge: a fine musician, an excellent warrior and leader of men, a superb politician, a king who accomplished much for his people. His sins, too, were big. He not only committed blatant adultery but had the woman's husband discreetly murdered. His gigantic capacity for all of life makes David the greatest of all Israel's kings. And his single-minded drive to serve the Lord as well as he could deserves our deepest respect.

David was the second king of Israel. The first had been Saul, who became insane and did unfortunate things, such as jealously hunting David all over the country to kill him. Before Saul, Israel had been governed by the judges. But the people began to want a more stable government like their neighbors had. With much reluctance, the Lord allowed Samuel the prophet to found a monarchy (1 Samuel 8). Since Saul failed in his main task, to secure the country militarily, David became the first king of a united nation. In fact, David's Israel was almost an empire, so large was the territory he controlled.

Because of David's power over so much land and so many people, it was important to Israel that he be dedicated to the

Lord. Israel thought of him as their central, necessary connection to God. Without him, they believed, the nation would lose its vitality because King David was its channel for God's life. So it became important that King David remain safe. After the kingdom was secure, he no longer went into battle but tended to administration and, probably, to liturgy. David's reputation as a psalmist probably has some factual basis, but also draws its strength from his founding of a school of liturgical music. There was as yet no temple, for the Lord had directed that Solomon, David's son, was to build the temple.

One might think that since David was so many-talented, he had no troubles. Not so! His troubles were like everything else: huge! He had trouble with a wife (Michal, Saul's daughter), troubles with sons who revolted against him (especially Absalom), troubles with court intrigues involving even his official prophet Nathan, and troubles with rivalries in his armies. Yet, David kept on striving to serve God and to do all he could for his people. In the end, he was the king closest to God who created a unified Israel. He is the greatest of the very few kings who are approved of in the Bible!

How can we learn from such a great person? He seems beyond us. Still, we can imitate his firm dedication to the service of the Lord. As he served in his big, history-making place, so we can serve in our smaller, less-famous places. Only a few people may see our service to God or others, but God will know — and he's the only one who counts.

We can also imitate David's willingness to fulfill his potential. He lived with enthusiasm and verve. He was not afraid to make mistakes nor to mourn for them when he finally recognized them. He was a *real* person. Everything he was shone out for all to see and share. He hid nothing. He did not live a small life, stuck in a corner of fear or feelings of unworthiness. He was fully whatever he was. He accepted responsibility for himself and lived boldly.

Such a person can bring so much more to God. When someone is ready to be all that he or she was created to be, then God has a larger, more available instrument for his purposes.

Is it risky to be that kind of person? Certainly. It requires courage and a zest for living. Such people are bound to be disliked by some. They will surely make mistakes and feel the consequences of bold choices. On the other hand, when a person hides his or her life in a safe corner, unwilling to share it generously and honestly, that life is wasted. Jesus told a parable about people like that. (You may read it in Luke 19:11-27.) The result of the waste is more frightening than any mistake could be.

Life and personal opportunities do not stand still. Not ever. If we are not stepping bravely forward to be all we can be, out front for all to see, then we will be moving backward by default, getting smaller and weaker inside. Finally, the marvelous potential in every one of us will disappear.

Thank God, the Bible gives us David to look at. We will not want to copy his obvious errors, but we can imitate his courage and his honesty with himself and others. We can *extend* ourselves boldly to life — and life will enrich us in return.

In the next few days, why not give yourself a treat? Read the whole story of David. A Bible dictionary will help in some places, but the story is good by itself — as good as any novel. Just be open to enjoying David, and let the Scripture itself bring you to insight.

7. ELIJAH

Elijah's Story: 1 Kings 17:1—19:21, 21:1-29; 2 Kings 1:1—2:11; Sirach 48:1-12

If Moses was the greatest of the Old Testament messengers from God, Elijah runs a close second. Although we have little recorded about Elijah, what we do have reveals a man of astounding strength and nearness to God. Tradition calls him the greatest of the prophets. Yet, even he had to *learn* to know God. His growth offers enticing clues for our living.

Elijah lived almost 250 years after David. He was the first of those we call the "classical" prophets. That word refers to those prophets (most of the biblical ones) who were not finders of lost things or judges in disputes, but who were called to speak forth God's Word in a particular time. Sometimes they predicted events too, but their main call was to communicate God's immediate message. It was never easy. It always made great demands on the prophet. The people were seldom receptive.

Elijah was impassioned for the Lord. He was determined to prove to the by now strangely obstinate Israelites that Yahweh (their name for the Lord) was, in fact, Lord of nature as well as law. If they could *get* that, it would end their troubles about other gods. Elijah strode over the land, proclaiming and convincing, confronting even the weak-kneed king and his thoroughly pagan queen.

In his most dramatic effort, Elijah challenged the prophets of the fertility god Baal. (The moviemakers have missed a great chance here — read it for yourself. It's terrific drama!) Elijah's contest was designed to demonstrate that Yahweh controlled nature. Drought already gripped the land because almost no one worshiped Yahweh alone. So, atop Mount Carmel on Israel's northern coast, Elijah and his single servant faced Baal's prophets. Queen Jezebel's men got first chance. They built an altar, prepared the sacrifice, and begged their god for fire. They chanted, gashed themselves, danced, and pleaded, while Elijah taunted them. No fire came. Finally, they tired, and it was Elijah's turn. He built an altar, prepared the sacrifice, drenched everything thoroughly, looked up to heaven and said, "Lord, answer me!" FIRE! And lots of it!

To eliminate the worship of Baal, Elijah then slaughtered the 450 Baalist prophets. Next, he sent word to King Ahab to gather up his picnic and head for home because it was going to rain at the word of the Lord. And so it did. It was a great victory.

But Jezebel was enraged. She put a price on Elijah's head. Suddenly, he felt afraid. He fled into the desert. He had done everything he could do, and it had gotten him exactly nowhere. He was discouraged enough to die. So he *gave up.* But then — after this extremity — Elijah experienced his most intense, intimate, and direct contact with God (1 Kings 19:8-18). Then, and only then, Elijah's work began to bear lasting fruit.

All Elijah's fervor, his extraordinary power and daring — all were ineffective until he let go of everything. Notice that he didn't let go because he was virtuous. He let go because he was tired, sad, and not a little mad. He was facing failure.

Most of us are like that. We cling hard to our projects and our good works for God. Only when we are exhausted or hopeless or helpless do we let go so God can do what he wants to do. When we put too much of ourselves into the action, even with excellent motives, our effort may come to nothing. When we give it all up, God's power can come through; and things begin to happen.

Elijah's desire for the Lord to rule the hearts of the Israelites was total. His deep desire was necessary. But total desire is only half of the condition needed for something to happen. The other half, which Elijah (like us) learned the hard way, is relinquishing the very thing we totally desire. A mother may beg for the life of her sick child, and prayers go on and on; but the child may die. Occasionally, however, the mother lets the child go into the loving will of God, and then his healing flows freely. Letting go heals the mother's spirit, and the child may get well also. It seems to be a constant: when we desire something truly good with all our hearts and then let go, the loving power of God takes over and all is made whole. It is a secret of effective prayer.

God is always ready to act. Are we ready to get out of his way and let him?

Here's an experiment for you. In a quiet time, prayerfully seek one of your own deepest desires. Pour out your desire to God. If you can do anything toward its accomplishment, by all means do it. Then, write your desire on paper and make a symbolic act of giving it to the Lord. You may seal it in an envelope and put it in your Bible or behind a picture. Pray, giving it to the Lord completely. Let it go. Then, mark on your calendar a date eight months to a year from now, reminding yourself to open the envelope on that day. You will likely be delightfully surprised! Rejoice then and praise God for his constant attention to you!

8. AMOS AND HOSEA

The Prophets' Stories ──────────────────────────

    In full: Amos 1—9; Hosea 1—14
   In brief: Amos 5, 6, 8; Hosea 1—3, 11, 14

About 100 years after Elijah, God sent two more prophets with a new task: proclamation without miracles. But, like Elijah, they were to announce the special Word of the Lord to his people Israel in their particular situation. As the 300-plus years since David had passed, the political situation had changed. Civil war had divided the Israelites into two countries: Israel, the northern kingdom, and Judah, the southern kingdom. (The whole people still called themselves "Israel" though.) The two prophets, Amos and Hosea, were both sent to the northern kingdom, whose capital was Samaria and whose chief shrine was Bethel.

The divisions had become religious as well as political, and the people in the north were deeply entangled in the worship of Baal and other fertility gods. Often, they included Yahweh; but they misunderstood him as one of the others. And so the Lord's Word became a Word of severe judgment, even condemnation and coming destruction.

Amos was the first of these two prophets. His message called the people urgently to return to God by returning to justice. For the Hebrews, justice didn't mean simply "getting what you deserve." It meant creating a situation in which each part of a society could live in harmony with all other parts. Amos insisted that only this dynamic justice would fulfill God's covenant with Israel.

In 5:12 Amos accuses Israel of
oppressing the just, accepting bribes,
    repelling the needy at the gate.

The gate in the city wall was used as the court of law in Palestinian cities, so we see that even legal proceedings were corrupt. And most abhorrent to the Lord, according to Amos, is the combination of living evily and worshiping God. The life makes the worship false.

I hate, I spurn your feasts,
    I take no pleasure in your solemnities. ...
Away with your noisy songs! (5:21-25)

Instead, the Lord begged them to forget about liturgy until they could

... let justice surge like water,
    and goodness like an unfailing stream.

If Israel continued in its materialistic ways and kept its false worship, the consequences would be grim:

I will forgive them no longer.
The temple songs shall become wailings. ...
    Many shall be the corpses,
        strewn everywhere. — Silence! (8:2,3)

Amos is not altogether pleasant reading. The Lord's accusations sound too much like conditions in the twentieth-century United States. Is his word for us? Will the Lord's consequences be as terrible for us as they were for Israel? All that Amos predicted came true within thirty years. Those people who are striving today to create social justice by definite action have heard clearly the message of Amos and other prophets. They call all of us to go to God with our whole hearts and just lives. Do we hear? Will we heed?

Hosea's message was like Amos', but with two differences. First, his message was lived out in his very flesh. Hosea had married and had three children. But his wife deserted them all to become a prostitute in the fertility temple of Baal. She violated not only their marriage but everything Hosea stood for as a servant of Yahweh. Then God required him to buy her back, discipline her, and reinstate her as his wife and the mother of his children — and through it all to love her!

As Hosea obeyed the Lord, in agony, he learned a central truth that makes him different from Amos. He learned that the Lord loved Israel through all her disobedience and carelessness toward him. However, God's love was not sentimental. It was what we call today "tough love." It meant that the consequences of Israel's disregard for the Lord would be terrible: their king and houses would disappear, thistles would grow in place of altars, and life would be so bad that the people would cry out to the mountains to fall on them (Hosea 10:7,8).

But the purpose of such terror is loving discipline. Afterward, the Lord can draw his people back to him with tenderness, because then (and only then) they will want God and respond to him. The destruction is to make people notice that they need their covenant Lord. After pages of complaints about Israel's thorough corruption, Hosea pleads,

Return, O Israel, to the LORD, your God

and the Lord promises,

I will love them freely. . . .

I will be like the dew for Israel:

he shall blossom like the lily (14:2-6).

Such a love is painful. Any parent who has a wayward child will understand Hosea's struggle and the anguish of Hosea's God. He is our God, too. Do we feel divine agony over the evils of our day? Do we accept his justice as readily as we do his tenderness?

After you read these two prophets, you may want to do something for justice. First, look carefully at your own participation in liturgy: do you pray while not caring about injustice, racism, the poor? If so, you can make a change there. If your life would respond to Amos' and Hosea's — and the Lord's — message, then perhaps you can volunteer to help those who are working full time for a just society. And let us remember to praise God always for his justice as well as for his undeserved, reliable love.

9. ISAIAH OF JERUSALEM

Isaiah's Work

In full: Isaiah 1—12, 31:1-3, 32, 36—39
In brief: Isaiah 1:1-13, 5:1—8:20, 31:1-3

Everyone who loves Scripture soon finds favorite passages which always have a certain power to touch the heart. Isaiah 6:1-13 is such a favorite for many. Here is the core of Isaiah's prophetic self-understanding, captured in his powerful, personal experience of God. He was in the temple. Many of the features of his experience (throne, seraphim, smoke) were physically present. But in the intensity of his experience, they were transformed and became messengers of God to Isaiah. His awareness centered on the holiness of God — an awareness so complete that the very decorations on the temple wall seemed to call it out aloud. So magnificent was the praise of God's holiness that the temple trembled.

Isaiah of Jerusalem worked from about 740 B.C. until sometime after 701 B.C. His work is recorded in most of Isaiah 1—39. For him, "holy" meant totally separate, totally other; either made separate by the nature of things or when God or people had consecrated something, separating it and making it sacred. God was holy in himself, utterly separate and sacred to humankind. Isaiah experienced the vastness of God's sacredness, and it changed his life forever.

First, he saw his own unworthiness and cried out that he was doomed. In his humility he was cleansed. Even more powerfully, he realized how corrupt his society was. He began to preach only a few years after Amos and Hosea, but in the southern kingdom of Judah. About halfway through his ministry, the northern kingdom (Israel) was captured by Assyria, and its capital Samaria was destroyed. All the strong people in the north had been scattered throughout the Assyrian Empire and replaced by natives loyal to Assyria. So Isaiah spoke to a nation seriously threatened by a huge and mighty empire at its very borders.

In Jerusalem, too, society was unjust, and worship of other gods was strong. Isaiah likewise cried out for justice and right worship, but he understood that justice was grounded in Yahweh's holiness. God's holiness expressed itself in justice, as Isaiah says in 5:16,

... God the Holy shall be shown holy by his justice.
Injustice was a direct violation of God himself.

God's holiness also implied his reliability and trustworthiness. Isaiah knew the nation could trust God and only God. He preached directly to the king that the country's salvation would come from quiet trust in the Lord and not from military struggle (7:2-9) nor from alliances with other mighty nations (31:1-3). Isaiah asked the king to trust firmly in God and to ask for a sign of the certainty of God's protection, but King Ahaz refused both. Isaiah replied by giving the sign from the Lord anyway, assuring King Ahaz that because of his refusal to trust God the sign would be for destruction and terror instead of security and goodness. It is no small thing to refuse to trust the Holy One!

Today it is harder to confront the government with the Word of the Lord. But God's ways are consistent; and Isaiah's message is that a nation should trust in God for its security, and not in arms or foreign alliances. How many of us trust God enough to even think of disarming and waiting in firm faith for God's action? Yet, that is precisely the implication of Isaiah's inspired speech to King Ahaz and of Isaiah's deep knowledge of God's holy reliability.

Isaiah challenged the king as representative of all the people. It was the whole people who needed to change their attitude toward the Holy One, and consequently their decisions about society's patterns too. Isaiah lived under a very different government from ours, but he was thoroughly political. For this prophet, if political realities did not express the will of the Holy One, they would draw certain destruction upon the whole society.

Isaiah did not speak to individuals as such because the individual hardly existed in the Hebrew mentality. Their sense of identity was firmly rooted in the group, the whole people. Today we listen more for the Word of the Lord to individuals. So, we may ask ourselves whether we trust God for security and peace in our own living — or do we trust more in the paycheck or the cost of living index?

Isaiah knew God's reliability because he had experienced God's holiness. We may never have such intense experience, but we can fix our attention on God, the Holy One, in our prayer. Psalm 89:1-9 is an excellent beginning for our prayer as we read Isaiah's work. And his work can, at the very least, increase a sense of urgency about our relationship to God. We can look through our self-examination to his perfection, his sacredness, his trustworthiness. We can praise him. Out of our praise may come a desire to respond more consistently to his ways and a willingness to trust him faithfully for all our needs. Let us fill ourselves with his praise!

10. JEREMIAH

Jeremiah's Work

In full: Jeremiah 1:1—2:37, 5:1-31, 11:1-14, 15:10-21, 20, 22:1-9, 31—45

In brief: Jeremiah 1:1—2:37, 5:1-31, 15:10-21, 30:8-24

So rich is the Book of Jeremiah (like Isaiah) that it would take many pages to barely outline it. Jeremiah lived in a complex and tragic time in Judah, about 100 years after Isaiah. He participated in all its troubles from the country's center, the court and temple in Jerusalem. His life was filled with suffering, his message was filled with condemnation and, in the short run, with failure. As with Amos, Hosea, and Isaiah, Jeremiah preached to a stubborn people who did not heed the Word of the Lord to them. He witnessed the final destruction of Judah and the demolishing of the temple amid ruined Jerusalem. He saw his people exiled into Babylon.

Yet, to Jeremiah came some of God's clearest promises, including the New Covenant (31:31-34) to be fulfilled six centuries later in Jesus Christ. To him also came the severest condemnations of Judah's worship of other gods. Jeremiah's life made possible a new understanding of the relationship between God and an individual. It is this that we want to understand a little better.

For centuries in Israel, the whole people had been the center of a person's identity, as mentioned before. Aside from the group, one had little sense of personhood. We can see this even today in some tribal societies. Jeremiah shared this view of himself, but he was wrenched out of it by his prophetic work. Because he lived through serious political upheaval and eventual destruction, as Judah fought for its existence, his preaching of Yahweh's Word of threatened exile hardly made him popular. He did not marry, and even his own family eventually rejected him. He had only a loyal secretary, Baruch, and a few benefactors who saved his life when he had been condemned. But, in effect, the only personal relationship Jeremiah had was with the Lord.

So, Jeremiah was virtually isolated. He suffered under this more than you or I might today. He suffered especially because he had no way of thinking about himself alone before God. He was part of a people; yet, he was called to be against them, filled with God's threats and condemnations. He felt torn in half by this result of his divine call to prophesy, for he was a keenly sensitive man.

Finally, Jeremiah complains bitterly to God and begs for vindication before his fellow Israelites (Jeremiah 15:10-21). God's answer is an insistence that Jeremiah repent! What can this mean to a man who has already lost everything valuable in his life for the sake of the Lord? It must have meant for Jeremiah that he quit complaining and that he accept the word and work of the Lord in full responsibility *as an individual* before him. Jeremiah must abandon any inward identity with his people and turn to God alone, willingly, for his personal life — a stunning requirement. He must also be stripped to his core of anything that was not of God, so that with his *whole* self he could turn to God. When that purification was completed, God promised to be continually present to Jeremiah and to deliver him. It was profoundly painful, but it brought to us humans a clearer self-understanding. It was a necessary step toward becoming fully human and responsible before God.

Today, we have over-stressed our individual identity to the exclusion of sensitivity to the people to whom we belong, and to our shared history as well. Even so, we do not always accept full responsibility before God. We blame the psychology of our parents, the faultiness of our education, the TV, Madison Avenue, and a dozen others for our weaknesses and lacks. We easily ignore our gifts and God-given capacities. What does responsibility mean for us?

First of all, we need to stop blaming everyone else for what we are, to admit accountability for the daily choices we make and for the quality of life we have. We need to see our weaknesses clearly and just as clearly to accept the loveliness in us. We need, simply, to be thoroughly honest with ourselves. Second, we need to admit our dependence on God. We cannot be anything that he desires unless we actively lean on him for our needs, securities, fulfillments. Third, we need to develop our fullest spiritual potential. That means, in the beginning at least, detachment from all that is small or unhealthy or selfish or other than God. It is a lifetime task, but it contains our glorious possibility as God made us to be — like himself! The process — like Jeremiah's — will hurt. The result will be splendid.

The twin of responsibility is freedom. As we become responsible before God, we become freer to know him. That's the gift which came to Jeremiah in his later years. Jeremiah paid heavily to live this freedom and to know God, since his circumstances were so terrible. Because of him, we have a more direct way to God. Let us be grateful to God for Jeremiah's faithful courage.

11. "DEUTERO-ISAIAH"

The Story

In full: Isaiah 40—55
In brief: Isaiah 40, 44, 49, 55

Did you ever, as a child, wish for something, dream about it, imagine having it, want it for a long time? And then, when someone finally gave it to you did it suddenly seem less attractive? Something like that happened to the Israelites on a grand scale, and the prophet we call Second, or "Deutero," Isaiah (because we don't know his name) was right in the middle of it all.

In 587 B.C. Jerusalem and Judah had been destroyed by Babylon, and Solomon's magnificent temple demolished. All but the weakest Israelites were deported into exile in Babylon, where they mourned lost homes, families killed, and the terrifying end of a whole way of life. They suffered especially the feeling that Yahweh had deserted them or even been defeated by the Babylonian god Marduk. Fifty years passed, and a whole generation of Hebrews grew up in Babylon. Finally, Yahweh again sent his Word to his exiled people.

This time, Second Isaiah was its channel. This prophet stood in the tradition of the first Isaiah of Jerusalem, but he spoke to a people in totally different circumstances. It was about 540 B.C. and destruction was behind them. The Hebrews lived not too uncomfortably in Babylon, but the news from Jerusalem was never good — it had become almost a home for scavengers.

The adult generation had never seen Palestine or Jerusalem. Still, their hearts yearned for God; and they felt they could never find him in Babylon. So they were worshiping other gods because they felt Yahweh had no power or no interest in them. Isaiah's message from the Lord was to comfort his people, then to convince them that he was still powerful and that he still cared for them. Isaiah was to announce that Cyrus, who had conquered nearby countries, would overthrow Babylon soon and that he would allow the Hebrew exiles to return home, for he was the instrument of Yahweh (unknown to himself). Cyrus would even provide from his treasury to help rebuild the temple. (See Isaiah 40 and 44.)

Chapters 40—55, the prophet's own writing, are especially beautiful even in English translation. Yahweh announces that he will make everything possible for his people to return to Jerusalem by an easy way. Isaiah proclaims that Yahweh is *all*-powerful because he is the Creator, the *only* God. He proves his point by showing how Yahweh, long before, had predicted all the terrors of the exile. Now he was predicting again, and this too would come true: Yahweh would bring them back to Jerusalem in peace. In 43 and 49:14-16 Isaiah reassures the exiles that God does indeed care intensely for them.

So, everything was prepared for the people to obey the Lord, and this time on a happy task: to return to Israel and to rebuild his holy temple. But like all the earlier prophets, Second Isaiah met with failure in his own time. Only a few people went home. Once again, most of the people didn't believe God and didn't obey him. Why?

We can only guess at their reasons: a big job ahead, a home already in Babylon, perhaps economic security, only their parents' memories to go on. But if human hearts are alike, even across centuries, the biggest reason may have been that they would have had to *trust* God, to believe that what he says is true and will be true — and act on that trust. It *is* difficult. After Jesus Christ as before him, we humans are reluctant to step very far beyond our own experience and our own sight.

Yet, God — in 2,000 years of our biblical history and 2,000 more years since Jesus — has never proved untrustworthy. He always has done what he said he would do. Those few who have risked trusting him and changed their lives accordingly have found inner riches of joy and peace that the rest of us only wonder about. Those few know that he wants our trust only for our own sakes. We are created for intimate communion with him, to be expressions of his life in our world. Nothing less will ever satisfy us. But it's so easy for us to be scared into thinking that we know better.

Second Isaiah's work was, like all the prophets' messages, significant at several levels. If we take Second Isaiah not only as historical but also as spiritual, we have a powerful call to inner growth. If, as the old poem says, "Heaven is my home, I'm just a stranger here," we are all called to *return*, to journey back to God. The way is prepared by God himself, and our arrival is assured if we want it. Shall we go together?

Only a few of the Israelites were present when the new temple was dedicated. Cyrus had kept Isaiah's promise, and the people who did return had worked hard. The dedication marked the beginning of a very important time in Israel, when the Bible was collected and put into its final inspired forms. But only a few were there. When God's promises to his people are fulfilled again, will we be there?

12. JOB

"She has the patience of Job." What a familiar expression! We all know it refers to a person who, in pain, is quiet and uncomplaining, who bears troubles without protest. But anyone who reads the Book of Job in the Bible must wonder how the expression ever began; because, although he does suffer greatly, Job is by no means quiet. In fact, he complains fiercely for over thirty chapters!

The Book of Job is almost unique in the Bible. It is not a historical report of actual events nor is it designed for liturgy nor does it record the work of prophets. It is more like a discussion of a very thorny problem put into story form. Hebrews loved stories, and they told stories to pass on their faith and culture from one generation to the next. Job probably began like that, for there is much evidence that it was not written all at once. It was included in the Bible because the Jews, and later the Christians, recognized its inspired quality.

As we now have the story, we are first introduced to Job, who is completely righteous and therefore blessed with all good things. Then we go to the heavenly court, where the angels are gathered before God. Satan (an angel whose special task is testing human beings; the word *satan* means "adversary" in Hebrew) wants to test Job, because he says anybody would be good if he got as much reward for it as Job has. So, God allows him first to destroy Job's property and family and, in the second round, to give Job horrible boils all over his body. Job goes into total mourning down in the town dump, but he does nothing sinful. (See chapters 1 and 2.)

Then Job is visited by three "friends," and here begins the main part of the Book. Together, they discuss his sufferings. The "friends" represent views common among Hebrew teachers. In between their speeches, Job speaks.

The "friends" argue something like this: We all know that righteousness is rewarded and evil is punished; therefore, Job must have some serious hidden evil in his life to have been so afflicted. The best thing for Job to do is to admit his evil and cast himself in repentance on the mercy of God. He should even be glad for his sufferings because God will deliver him. But Job repeatedly insists that he has done no evil thing and has no evil in his heart. The "friends" say his protest itself is evil. In all his argument, Job never blasphemes God; but he does complain that in all justice this should not have happened to him. Finally, Job tires of the discussion and appeals directly to God, demanding that God hear his complaint and himself judge whether he has not been unjust in Job's case.

The Lord's answer explains nothing. God communicates directly to Job. Job experiences God in his power as Creator. He realizes that only God is wise; only God is powerful; only God really knows or does anything righteous or significant. Job is overwhelmed:

I am of little account . . .
    I put my hand over my mouth (40:4).

His experience deepens, and Job realizes more and more what God is and how little Job is. He says:

I had heard of you by word of mouth,
    but now my eye has seen you.
Therefore I disown what I have said,
    and repent in dust and ashes (42:5-6).

The story's final touch is very satisfying to us: the "friends" are rebuked by the Lord, and everything that Job lost is given back to him.

But somehow we may feel we have no answer to the Book's questions about suffering. God does not explain it in a way our minds can grasp. Job's peace does not come from an answer — it comes from his experience of God. Is that enough for us?

Centuries of saints have testified that God — and only God — is abundant fulfillment, no matter what else one does or does not have. They say even suffering becomes insignificant in the midst of any direct experience of God. Before Job's experience of the Lord, he was honest and kept searching and called for God's reply. He was given no answer. He was given God himself.

Perhaps that can suggest a direction for us when suffering visits us. Let's not decide that God is terrible or that he is powerless. Let us not *blame* God. Let us, rather, stay honest (God *is* God — and we do not understand), open our feelings to God, and seek God with all the intensity of our pain. That's certainly not easy to do. It may not explain why things are the way they are, for the workings of the universe are God's not ours. But it could bring us closer to God as he is. As you reflect on Job, take your pain into your prayer as Job did: feel free to complain to God and search for what you need, but most of all beg for God himself. In him alone is all our peace to be found.

13. PROVERBS

Read Proverbs at random.
Don't miss: 1:1-7, 8, 31:10-31.

Once, two college boys had a contest. One searched the Bible and the other searched Shakespeare for a whole summer to see which of them could find the greatest number of familiar quotations. It was almost a tie, and the boys were astounded at their discoveries. "A soft answer turns away wrath" (see 15:1). "The fear of the Lord is the beginning of wisdom." (see 1:7). "Pride goes before a fall" (see 16:18). These are from Proverbs, and you will find many more when you look for yourself.

The Book of Proverbs is a collection of sayings, written and kept by Hebrew teachers across several centuries. We call these teachers the "wise men" or the "Wisdom School." (They were mentioned before in the chapter on Joseph.) We know very little about them except by comparison with countries around Israel, where "wise men" were experts in writing and often hired by kings to keep records and take down laws and messages. But "wise men" were also experts in observing life about them. Some of their observations are in the Bible, in the "Wisdom Books," including Proverbs, Job, Ecclesiastes, Wisdom, and Sirach. In Proverbs we find some sayings which make us smile at their accuracy: "He who blesses his neighbor with a loud voice, rising early in the morning, will be counted as cursing" (see 27:14). We also find serious advice:

Trust in the LORD with all your heart,
  on your own intelligence rely not ...
  and he will make straight your paths (see 3:5,6).

It is sheer delight to go exploring in Proverbs. The collection seems to have little particular order that we can find, so it's excellent for browsing. As we read, we find a kind of pattern in the sayings. A statement is made and then, usually, right away another that re-states the original idea from a slightly different angle, or states the opposite. Either way, the main idea becomes clearer and fuller with the second part.

Think about the Proverbs that especially strike you as you read. Do they match your own experience or your observations of how things work in your world? Many of them do, for the original writers were careful to reflect on what they saw and to give advice about how a good life can be lived. You may want to apply them to yourself or your family and friends. (Keep a light touch though!) One person even made a party out of Proverbs. She made a poster of an apple tree, with a Proverb behind each apple. Each person chose an apple, read the Proverb aloud, and shared what it suggested to him. Out of this game came a lot of fun, some suggestions for growth, and shared prayer as well. Then the hostess served cupcakes — and each one had a Proverb wrapped in foil and baked right into it.

The intention of Proverbs is serious, however. The Hebrews believed in seeking Wisdom. They thought of Wisdom as being very close to God, almost divine, and very important to the life of the world (chapter 8). Wisdom was important to individuals, for she guided men in their decisions and warned them of dangers. Wisdom gave necessary guidelines for living fully and beautifully, with as little trouble as possible. Wisdom helped people to be fully human. Young people were urged to love Wisdom and seek her out and respond to her teaching. For some this meant becoming pupils in the Wisdom School and learning to observe life and submit to life's teaching.

This viewpoint — that of learner of Wisdom — is often lost among us. Particularly in America we like to write our own rules for living and call it freedom. But, according to the Bible and, especially, the Wisdom Books, that is a false attitude. The rules for living are built into our world, our daily experience — if we but look for them. They were put there by God. The truly wise person will follow those principles and let them guide his or her decisions and activities. Only in this way, the ancient Hebrews knew, can life be as full as we want it to be. Only in this way can we truly understand what life is.

Proverbs may seem, at first glance, an easy Book. It certainly is not as hard to understand as the prophets. But living according to those Proverbs is not so easy. They often describe behavior which we instantly see is good but which we must make an effort to practice. Or they describe action which is the result of long discipline and attentive choice. You may want to discover the real depth of Proverbs by choosing one or two and making them your "rules of life" for a few weeks. Surprises are likely!

Writing *true* Proverbs is also not easy — but it can be an interesting project. You may want to try it. You must follow basic rules, though: observe something about your life, write it in as few words as possible, then write a second side of your observation which enhances the first. This experiment will sharpen your awareness of living, and it will be enjoyable too.

14. ECCLESIASTES

"Vanity of vanities! All is vanity," says the Preacher, Qoheleth. Again he says, "There is nothing new under the sun." Few of us would agree. We believe that our experiences and activities are important and not vanity. We believe in progress, too, and anyone who saw pictures of humans walking on the moon would surely say there is something new under the sun. Yet, the Preacher *is* Holy Scripture. What can we make of it?

I've known two people who claimed their favorite biblical Book was Ecclesiastes. One was a woman highly educated but old and sick, facing death. The other was a young man serving a life sentence in state prison. Both suffered very much. What did they find in this Book?

As with all Scripture, we must look to the inner qualities of things to appreciate our ancient Preacher. He was one of the Wisdom School, and he carefully observed human life as he saw it before him and felt it in himself. He looked at riches and pleasure, at work and its results, at evil and retribution, and at human ignorance in all life's events. He looked for order and the action of God in everything.

Qoheleth found that everything was sent by God (2:24) for reasons we cannot determine or understand. He learned that underneath our human busyness God has created an order (3:10-15) with a certain timeliness and a stability that lasts. God remains in mystery while ordering this earth and the lives of people so that we may learn reverence for him.

The greatest gift of God, says the Preacher, is mirth and enjoying "with the wife whom you love" whatever good things life offers. Nothing else has *any* value, and even this is limited (9:7-10). But in the end it is only moments of enjoyment that count — because one *cannot* know the big answers.

What can hurting people find here? One possibility is relief from ambition. Most of us are driven people: we strive to achieve and accomplish; we push ourselves to know and to prove what we know; we work as if there is nothing else to do; and we are determined to control all things on the earth. To all this, Qoheleth would exclaim, "Vanity of vanities — a chasing after wind!"

There is a large peace to be found in his attitude: there are wars and troubles, there have always been wars and troubles; there are achievements and failures, there have always been achievements and failures; the cycle of human life goes around and around, and only God knows the reasons. If one has suffered sharply, one can see that this is a fair description of the way things are — and a trip to the moon makes very little difference in the human round of daily living and daily struggles. So what is one to do? Quit pushing, says Qoheleth. Be at peace and enjoy what comes your way.

The painful sense of one's own helplessness can bring us to see that there is nothing one can do to change the larger order of human existence. One could give up and despair, but the Preacher doesn't. He looks the mystery of God's earth directly in the face; and, although he can't explain it any better than you or I, he finds a certain inner contentment in it. He relaxes and discovers a great thing: the present moment.

Only a simple person can make peace and enjoyment in the present moment. Simplicity lets God be God and doesn't probe around overmuch in his affairs. It accepts our individual limitations and those of the race. It does not rail against what we cannot alter. Simplicity does and enjoys whatever comes to hand and leaves the grand results to God — as a willing worker does to the one in charge. Suffering can bring a person to this simplicity. Such simplicity is great wisdom.

The Preacher's final advice to us (11:9,10) is his word to the young: rejoice and follow your heart, not forgetting God's judgment, and avoid trouble. Perhaps if we left our passions and strivings for eternal progress, turned to God in acceptance, and rejoiced in the delights of the present moment, we would find a different and better peace than the one we expect achievement to bring. A heart contented in the streaming changes of life is a very great, and very rare, gift.

The Preacher's advice is worth some practice. Try it! Ignore your huge expectations and enjoy what each hour brings. The beauty in simple contentment may surprise you. And if you can't maintain it for long, remember it and return to it whenever you can.

15. DANIEL

The Daniel Stories

> **In full:** Daniel 1—14
> **In brief:** Daniel 1:1—3:97, 6:1—9:27, 13:1—14:22

Do you think of the lions' den when you hear of Daniel? Most people do; but if you are not sure what he was doing there, you can find it in chapter 6 of the Book of Daniel. It is one in a collection of stories about a man who lived close to God. The stories are delightful in themselves; but, like all biblical stories, they point beyond themselves to God and his relationship to human beings.

We do not know if Daniel was an actual person because there are many historical inaccuracies in the Book. We do know that the Book of Daniel was not written until around 165 B.C., some 400 years after the events described there. In any case, the stories are about a Daniel who lived in Babylon during the Exile. Other parts of the Book, like the visions, likely originated about the time the Book was written and were attributed to Daniel.

Here are the reasons for this arrangement. In the Exile, Hebrews were under constant pressure to conform to the customs, laws, and religion of the Babylonians. It was at times life-threatening to refuse to conform. But Daniel and his three close friends were faithful to the God of their fathers, the true God. Consequently, God gave them great wisdom and saved them from difficulties, including the famous lions' den. Four centuries later, the Jews were in Palestine, but political circumstances and cultural pressures were even worse than those in the Exile had been. An arrogant dictator ruled Judea and had no liking for his subjects or their God. He oppressed and destroyed the people when they would not submit to cultural (Greek) customs and ideas. The struggle became so intense that families were divided, even killing one another over their religious convictions. (Some of the history of this period is recounted in the Books of the Maccabees.)

In such horrible situations, great reassurance is needed by those who remain faithful. Such times often inspired "apocalyptic" writing. This is a special form of sacred literature which has a definite purpose: by visions and symbols, it shows the events of present and future as an earthly version of a spiritual conflict. The winner in this battle is always God, who stands by his faithful people. The loser is always the oppressive power. So the faithful are strengthened to be loyal and wait for God's action. The visions of Daniel were just such an apocalyptic encouragement. By attributing them to the ancient Daniel in Babylon, the writer (of 165 B.C. or so) could hide his identity. By writing in a visionary style, full of symbols and code words, he could communicate with his community without revealing the message to the "other side."

The visions are largely puzzles to us because we are not familiar with the exact political circumstances nor with the symbolism itself. Historians have decoded some of the visions, however. Aside from the political issues of that distant time, the Book of visions (chapters 7—12) has an important message for us today: God rules history; nothing happens without his permission, and nothing happens that he does not eventually turn to his good purposes. God is trustworthy. We are commanded to trust him and remain faithful to him. That means keeping his principles for living, doing as he has urged us, and leaving all the results up to him. Such faithfulness is focused in Daniel 3:17-18, where three Jews are threatened with death in a furnace if they don't worship the Babylonian god. They reply, "If our God, whom we serve, can save us from the white-hot furnace and from your hands, O king, may he save us! But even if he will not, know, O king, that we will not serve your god. . . . "

In our country there is no *political* persecution of Christians. But our society is becoming less and less Christian in ways that are hard for us to untangle. It is often unclear just how to express our Christianity in today's world. We are asked almost daily to give allegiance to something less than God, to question God's power over our lives and over our history. Our society hardly helps us to be faithful to God. Most "up-to-date" values are not those of Jesus. This is a great challenge — and a very uncomfortable one. If we face it squarely, we may become "outsiders" in our own world. If we ignore the differences between twentieth-century Americanism and Christianity, we may well end up ignoring God. We have little choice about what the whole society is like. We can choose everything about how we live within it.

The message of Daniel is necessary for us. We are called by it to be faithful to God and his Son and, in the midst of a pagan society, to create life as God has directed through the Scripture and the Church. Our lives are too short to know the outcome, but we do know from Daniel that God is completely in charge. Kingdoms and societies come and go. God alone remains, and he is faithful to those who obey him. It couldn't have been easy for Daniel; it won't be easy for us. But we will have final security and peace in our hearts if we follow God.

16. LOOKING TOWARD CHRIST

Readings: Isaiah 9:1-6, 52:7-10, 62:1-5,11-12

The verses to be read with this chapter were written over a span of nearly 200 years, between 725 and 540 B.C. They were later included in the Book called Isaiah. The inspired words point forward to a special time in the history of God's people Israel and of the whole world. Since the beginnings of the Church, these passages have been taken to predict the coming of Jesus Christ. Today they still intrigue us.

The predictions do not mention specifics like the Bethlehem cave or Caesar's tax. Rather, they urge the hearer to expect certain qualities of life when the Savior comes. Joy and light stand out among the first of them. Right alongside is relief from burdens and from wars. These alone would be enough to bring great wonder to us. But there is more: the Savior will be a person of genuine authority, not political savvy. He can be trusted. He will be wise and full of love. He will bring tranquillity and power for living. All this will be his gift to people. But there is still more: the very news of his coming will be inexpressibly good; and people will sing songs of joy as they receive back all they have lost, plus comfort for the losing. All will be renewed as God delights in the Savior and his work.

We may have a little trouble taking it all in. Certainly, the ancient Hebrews who first heard the predictions found the glory of such promises little more than words — good words, hopeful words, but only words. The verses themselves seem to anticipate this human reaction, so they insist on God's determination to accomplish his promises. In Isaiah 9:6 we read:

The zeal of the LORD of hosts *will* do this!

"Lord of hosts" was one of the mightiest titles given to God by Israelites, establishing his power as commander of all the forces of the universe. And this mighty God is zealous — eager and determined — to act. In 52:10,

The LORD has bared his holy arm
in the sight of all the nations.

Even today the image of a strong man baring his arm is an image of power; it is action about to explode. In 62:11, "the LORD proclaims" again that he will bring his promises to fruition. His promises are not only words, though they begin with the power in words. They are qualities assured by God himself for the coming redemption.

That very assurance may puzzle us. Jesus the Savior did come; and, although we love him dearly, we look at our world and it hardly seems redeemed, or anyway is not full of the promised qualities. In fact, we know that in much of our world these qualities of the Savior's work are phantom dreams and that what dominates is more a spirit of fear and trouble. Has something gone horribly wrong?

God does not make mistakes. We know that. Yet, when we don't understand we may be tempted to think that God has somehow erred. But, if God makes no mistakes, the only others around who might are you, me, and the rest of humankind. That can be a pretty heavy burden. We are not able to shoulder it so readily. That is exactly why we need a Savior! It is exactly why we need to admit the Savior into our whole life, and not leave him only in church.

So, as we leave the Old Testament and go to the New, we may find it hopeful to look within ourselves once again. We may search out whether we are ready to welcome the Savior God sent. More exactly, we can discover how we *have* welcomed him and also how we have not.

In Isaiah 62:5, God uses the figure of a marriage to explain what he is going to do:

As a young man marries a virgin,
  your Builder shall marry you;
And as a bridegroom rejoices in his bride
  so shall your God rejoice in you.

God is ready for us — he has been for many centuries. But a marriage takes two. This two-ness is necessary for the promised qualities of God's prophecies to reach their fullest expression. If God is the Giver, we are the receivers; and only when the gifts are received are they fully given. God forces nothing — not even joy — upon us. So, if God is one partner in the "marriage," perhaps we can find ways to become more truly the other partner. Alone, no one person can be that whole partner. But as members of a community of faith in God's promises, we can. Then the "marriage" can take place so that all of those promises can be fulfilled, and our lives actually take on the qualities promised by the prophets, to be given through Jesus Christ.

Introduction to the New Testament

Readings: John 1:1-5, 20:30-31, 21:24-25
Romans 8:28-39
1 Corinthians 1:1-5
Revelation 5:7-13

In the first part of this book we have looked at the Old Testament. But the Old Testament is only part of our Scripture. Now it is time to look at the other part, the New Testament.

The Old Testament is the story of God's relations with his particular people, the Israelites. There God's Word is revealed in law, in prophecy, and in action. As years pass and the people respond (or do not respond) to God, they learn more about who he is and what he is like.

The New Testament tells of the Word of God made flesh in Jesus Christ. God expresses himself perfectly in and through Jesus so that he may be fully revealed to his people. But now "his people" are not only one nation. It includes all who choose to be Jesus' followers.

Four Books in the New Testament, the Gospels, are about Jesus' life on this earth. We also find Letters written by Paul and other early Christians. Here we discover what Jesus meant to those first disciples and what their experience of him was like. They knew him or knew someone who had known him. He had re-created their lives. The early Christians also meant a lot to each other. They were human and full of foibles but drawn closely together by Jesus Christ, so they were ready often even to die for one another.

The Gospel stories about Jesus and the experiences of the early Christian community are special to us. They are a light for our way and a fence to keep us from falling into too many deep pits! They can help us grow in our own experience of God and in our life with him.

The New Testament *seems* more familiar to us than the Old Testament. We have heard it oftener, and the culture seems less strange to us. We must not let such a familiar feeling lure us into indifference. The New Testament can be even harder to understand than the Old because it challenges us to a great depth in our living before God. We may even actually still be living in the Old Testament while trying to believe in the New! It is not enough to know historical facts about Jesus or about Paul. The New Testament invites us to go beyond head knowledge, to create a life-style based on Jesus Christ. Such an aim will never be easy. And genuine understanding may always be beyond us. Yet, to say "yes" to that invitation is the glory to which we are called and the promise toward which we walk.

These chapters on the New Testament will sketch something of its invitation, so we may see a little better the quality of life to which Jesus invites us. But the New Testament can help only if we are open to the experience described there, the experience of Jesus' love and, likewise, his challenge.

First, we will glance at John the Baptizer who prepared Jesus' way. We will look at a few main points from the Gospels — Jesus' teachings, his power, his Passion, and his invitation to union with himself and the Father. Then, we will think about Paul's reflection of Jesus' meaning to him and to other Christians. Paul also comments about the Christian communities as he knew them. Finally, to close the book as Scripture itself closes, we will take a quick look at the Book of Revelation — a puzzle in places, it is still a burst of utter confidence in the power of Christ.

Several readings are suggested above. As you ponder them, you will get a notion of what the New Testament says about itself. John says that the Word became flesh and that he writes only to encourage belief in Jesus Christ. Paul wonders aloud at the amazing love of Jesus Christ and the mercy of God which never depart from us, no matter what our circumstances are. On this unshakable conviction we can base our own "yes" to the invitation of the New Testament. Then, if we follow through, we can join the huge and splendid chorus of the Church through the ages, crying out, "Come, Lord Jesus!"

17. JOHN THE BAPTIZER

Readings: Luke 1:5-80, 3:1-20

When the President of the United States plans to visit another country, people are sent ahead of him. Security officers go to make sure of his safety. Protocol experts go to arrange for people to stand, sit, and greet the President. Personal staff go so he will be comfortable in his accommodations. No one of much importance ever simply shows up!

So, also, when God was to send his Son to visit humankind on earth, he sent John the Baptizer ahead to get things ready. The necessary readiness was not physical, however. It was a preparation of people's hearts, a spiritual readiness to receive Jesus Christ.

In the Gospel of Luke, the coming of Jesus is closely connected with the coming of John. Parallel events surround their births. An angel comes to Zechariah to announce that he will be the father of a boy, a special messenger from God (1:10-17). Likewise, an angel comes to Mary and announces that she will be the mother of a boy, *the* messenger, the Son of God (1:16-33). As Jesus was to be superior to John, so Mary's response in faith (1:38) was superior to Zechariah's skepticism (1:18).

Mary set out to visit Zechariah's wife, Elizabeth, to see the promised sign (1:36). On her arrival, she sings a canticle of praise, the *Magnificat* (1:46-55). Later, when John the Baptizer is born, Zechariah also sings a canticle of praise (1:68-79).

As an adult, John the Baptizer lived out his message. He went into the desert, where nothing could distract him from communing with God (1:80). Only at God's word did he wander along the Jordan River preaching God's message (3:2,3). Thus his life took the form of an ancient prophet's life, which his hearers knew very well from their tradition. By his life-style, John was unmistakably recognizable as a messenger from God.

John called his hearers to look carefully into their own lives. Those who needed attack to wake them up, he attacked, in the true prophetic tradition (3:7). Those who needed advice, he advised (3:7-14). To all he announced the necessity of changed attitudes and changed lives. He called them to "repent." That word does not mean beating one's breast in a spasm of misery. It means knowing one's real inner condition, one's own qualities and habits, deciding which need changing and then *doing* the changing.

John used another familiar form to seal his hearers' intention to change. Baptism was not invented by John. It was a ritual often used by the Jews to receive converts into Judaism. No Jew ever regarded himself as needing baptism; cleansing so radical was required only by Gentiles! So, everyone could see that John's baptism was a serious rite, suitable only for people who were changing — and radically — their lives.

All John's work was to prepare the people for the coming of one "who is mightier than I" (3:16). To do so, he cried out for change in the actual behavior of people. He was calling them back to a way of life closer to the Covenant way they often ignored or changed to suit their life-style. Thus, he was the connector between the Old Testament traditions and the age of Christ.

Cleansing and changing were necessary preparations because Jesus Christ was himself so much more, and was both to offer and to demand a far higher quality of life than whatever the people had known before. A person had to qualify himself inwardly to get ready for Jesus so as to be able to respond to him. John urged the people to do it.

Today, too, John calls us through the Scriptures to prepare ourselves to receive Christ more completely, for his coming is always more than we can absorb all at once. We must continue to change, to clean ourselves interiorly as well as outwardly. Every "clean" spot in us will be filled by Christ. Thus, Jesus continually comes into our lives, continually bringing us to richer, truer living.

If we want to follow John's urging, here are four steps we can take:

First, we can look at ourselves, our daily habits, the qualities we give expression to, and how closely we meet our ideals. We need to watch ourselves to *get information*. We need not evaluate at first. We need only notice, to try to see clearly. Most of us, most of the time, are so caught up in whatever we do that we hardly know what we *are* each day or each hour. But by observation we can learn.

Second, we can decide which of our habits and qualities we want to keep and which we want to let go. We will hold on to those which help us receive Jesus more deeply. This is decision-making for each one alone, thinking honestly before God.

Third, we can offer our positive qualities and habits to Jesus, asking him for a great filling with his Spirit. Even our very best selves can be transformed if the Spirit of Christ acts through them.

Fourth, we can offer to Christ those things we don't want to keep. We ourselves must make what changes we can. The rest will be changed as we leave them with him.

None of this heart preparation has to make us miserable. All self-knowledge is empowering, even if startling sometimes. We can be joyfully certain that Christ will fill our heart to the extent that we demonstrate our readiness and our desire to have him. By following John the Baptizer, we ready ourselves for the deeper coming of the Son, whose "mercy is from age to age" (1:50).

18. MIRACLES IN MARK

Readings: Mark 4:35-41, 6:34-52, 10:46-52

How can we know the will of God for us? How can we learn what Jesus Christ intends for us? Certainly, one way is through the Scriptures. Sometimes we limit God's possibilities even in the Bible because we think our question means: what does God want me to *do*? Sometimes it does mean that. But in Scripture another meaning is given equal time. That is, what does God want to give me?

For many, that is the harder question. Perhaps we have too long thought that "God's will" is only a large demand on us. But in the Bible, we see a God who gives, who takes the initiative in giving, and who always gives more than we could possibly return, or even ask for! Jesus gave to many people before he asked them to respond in any way. He gave freely, simply for love. The miracle stories in the Gospel of Mark show us, in Jesus' own action, that he wills us to receive from him.

In Mark 4:35-41 we find the familiar story of the storm on the Sea of Galilee, when Jesus slept in the boat. Terrified, his disciples awakened him. He calmed the winds and quieted the water. It was Jesus' will that the disciples should be protected from catastrophe. It is God's primary will for us, too. When we cry out for the protection we need, it is usually given to us — and sometimes quite dramatically. Christendom is full of personal experiences of God's protection.

God wants to protect us, but we must ask him and must expect — not merely wish for and not take for granted — results. We may think first of physical protection, such as is given in this story. But, more important, God also wants to protect us from spiritual dangers, especially the storms that sometimes rage in our inner selves. At times, all of us are full of emotions we cannot understand or confusion we cannot clarify. Think of the angers and guilts and fears that make our inner life tempestuous and frightening. In these, too, we can cry out for God's protection. It will be given. God wants us to receive his protection as gift. Let us remember to ask for it in our own stormy times.

In Mark 6:34-52 we read about Jesus feeding 5,000 people with a few loaves and fish. How awed that crowd must have felt as they slowly realized that they were being fed by more-than-ordinary means. Jesus had compassion on these people because they were hungry. He knew their hunger was physical and spiritual as well. So is ours. He wants to nourish us. This story is immediately followed by Jesus walking on the water, and the last verse says that his disciples "did not understand about the loaves." Perhaps, with 2,000 years of hindsight, we understand a little bit better.

Today, we do see that Jesus wants to nourish people. He wants all people to have the basic necessities for bodily life, especially food. He is able to provide food, particularly through the generous giving of other people. Moreover, in the Gospel, this story is understood to symbolize the Eucharist. Christ wants us to be fully nourished — physically and spiritually, eucharistically. How open are we to receiving his complete nourishment? If someone across town were passing out packets of $100 bills for an hour every morning, it wouldn't seem hard to get there, would it? Is the Mass as important? All of us can participate often and openheartedly in the Mass. All of us can pray that we allow him to free us however and whenever he chooses.

God also wants us to be whole. Everywhere Jesus went, he healed those who asked him. Wholeness implies not only bodily wellness or psychological health but also, and most important, spiritual growth. Christ's healing at every level is available to us, and it is his will that we receive it from him. If we believe we can do without him, then we will have to! We must want his wholeness and freedom to love, which Christ offers us. We must ask insistently, as did Bartimaeus in Mark 10:46-52. Bartimaeus was a blind beggar who wanted Jesus to heal him. When he cried out to Jesus his friends tried to hush him, but he only yelled louder and more persistently. Jesus heard. Jesus answered. Jesus healed.

Strangely, many people get attached to their pains and problems and do not open themselves to God's healing. It might be helpful to check ourselves and see if we do that. An open heart is a possibility for each one of us. But we must ask with more than words. We must ask with our choices, our presence, our actions, our deep desire. We must do what we know to do. Too often we ask only with words, and that seldom brings results. It is not *real* openness. It is closedness with a certain self-deception. That is contrary to God's will.

Jesus was and is a healer who wants to make us whole. He *knows* how much we need healing, but he cannot give it unless we ask with all our being and our strength. When we insist on being healed, by doing everything we can to open ourselves, Jesus will heal. He will touch first the most important sickness. There may be inner things that have to be whole before the body can be whole or before the person can be truly free. We can trust his action in us to be compassionate and knowledgeable. Every Gospel repeats over and over that Jesus heals because he wants us whole. Our question must be: do I want to become whole?

The Gospel of Mark shows Jesus working at his mission on earth. Jesus' mission to us includes the same works: to protect us, to nourish us, to heal us. It is God's will that we receive Jesus' work.

19. THE SERMON ON THE MOUNT

Readings: Matthew 5, 6, 7

If you were about to make an extended visit to outer space, you would be planning very carefully, wouldn't you? You would be training for the trip and learning about the conditions and laws prevailing at your destination. You would want to know as much as possible, before you took off, about "how things work out there."

A similar challenge is ours when we consider living in the Reign (or Kingdom) of God. Even though the Kingdom was the main subject of Jesus' preaching, we are often not clear about preparing ourselves to live there. Yet, Jesus assured his followers that God's Reign had come and all of us might live there *now.*

The Sermon on the Mount (the common name for chapters 5, 6, and 7 of Matthew's Gospel) is a collection of Jesus' sayings about life in the Reign of God *now.* They are not about heaven, although the Reign may indeed be completed then. These sayings are about earth. They teach us the conditions and principles of life *here* in God's Reign. If they sound a little strange, it is because the Reign of God *is* strange when compared to the values and customs of the world. We belong to that world, and we see things from its viewpoint. But we may also, if we wish, belong to the Reign of God. The Sermon on the Mount gives us descriptions of that life. Let's note especially that Jesus did not command anyone to live like this; he invited only, then offered these principles of "how things work in the Reign."

How does this understanding of the Sermon apply? Take the ordinary matter of money, food, and clothing. In 6:25-33, Jesus says, "Do not worry about your livelihood ... Your heavenly

Father knows all that you need." You know the rest about the birds and the lilies. It all sounds lovely — and impractical. But this is not instruction in *ordinary* living, it is instruction for *Reign of God* living. The key to not worrying about obvious needs is verse 33: "Seek first his kingship over you, his way of holiness, and all these things will be given you besides." That means exactly what it says: if I put the Reign of God first (a big if!), then God will provide all I need to live the way he wants me to live.

In the next few days, you might like to think about your present priorities. How high up is the Reign of God? Might it be adventuresome to put God's Reign first? What steps could you take toward that?

Another concrete principle Jesus offers is 7:12, the familiar "Golden Rule": "Treat others the way you would have them treat you." Many of us usually think of this as a law of charity. We assume that its primary purpose is the welfare of the "other guy." But that is a misunderstanding of Jesus' idea. In 7:2, Jesus gives the basis for the Golden Rule: "The measure with which you measure will be used to measure you." In other words, what you give is what you *will* get back. When that notion comes alive in us, we see that the Golden Rule is only good sense. We are its chief benefactors — it helps the "other guy" secondarily only.

The Golden Rule also gives a clue as to how we got where we are today. What we now have, especially within ourselves, tells us just how we have been living our lives. If we've been most interested in material things, giving time and effort and money to them, that is what we have. If our investments have been in relationships, then that's what we have. If we've been spreading kindness on the earth, it has returned to us, often from unexpected directions. If we poison the atmosphere around us, we poison ourselves as well.

Sometimes it takes courageous honesty to see that this principle has always been working in one's life. But it is worth it to take a look, because then we can turn things around if we wish. In the Reign of God we can have the quality of life we want by using this Rule, by *giving* what we ourselves desire. It is sometimes difficult because our ego-centered self forgets easily and wants to force results. But it is possible. It is up to us. Jesus forces no one. He only tells us how things work. This is one principle we can certainly try.

If you look attentively at your life in the light of these two challenges, your curiosity may lead you further. As you train yourself for the Reign of God, you will probably — like thousands before you — discover that you didn't know as much or were not quite as right as you imagined. Good! That is the first step, even though your pride is wounded and you may feel pretty bad at first. You can rejoice, because Jesus said (5:3) that the "poor in spirit" can be happy because the "reign of God is theirs." Being poor in spirit is exactly what we experience when we begin to know how far away from God we often are, when we feel our weaknesses, when we recognize that we haven't lived much in the Reign of God. It can break our hearts. Perhaps only then can God enter our hearts fully. Isn't that what we want?

So rejoice! One day Matthew 7:24-25 can be fully true: "Anyone who hears my words and puts them into practice is like the wise man who built his house on rock. When the rainy season set in, the torrents came and the winds blew and buffeted his house. It did not collapse. . . . "

20. UNION WITH CHRIST IN JOHN

Readings: John 14, 15, 16

When you were in love the very first time, you found yourself attracted by certain qualities in the other person. When you thought about uniting your lives, it probably was not the number of your agreements or the number of possessions or the amount of education either of you had that mattered most. You looked at the qualities of your proposed partner. Something in us knows that certain qualities make union with someone possible.

The same thing is true when we think about that awesome possibility: union with Jesus Christ. Union with him cannot come from the number of Masses we have shared, the number of rules we keep, or the amount of suffering we endure. Union with Christ can be grounded only in qualities within us, which our experiences, however, may contribute to.

In the Gospel of John, the writer tells us how we can find union with Jesus Christ. In chapters 14, 15, and 16, he gives us his memories and reflections of Jesus' last discussion with his closest followers. These chapters are called the Last Discourse and took place at the Last Supper, as this Gospel gives it to us. The main subject is the union of Jesus' followers within himself and with his Father.

Let's look at some qualities which Jesus says make for union with him. The first is found in 14:1: "Do not let your hearts be troubled. . . . " That challenge requires trust in God, and we can help ourselves develop this untroubled quality of heart:

1. We can put our worries into the hands of God and, then, think of other things and choose other emotions. If this is a new inner skill, it may seem awkward or artificial at first. But it is

possible, and the effort is fruitful. With practice, this inner act becomes a constant attitude. Then our hearts *are* less troubled.

2. We can avoid reading, discussing, or doing things which trouble us unnecessarily. Dwelling on the terrors in the news, talking about the faults of our acquaintances or family, being angry at people we hardly know — these are a few of the troubling habits we can avoid. If union with Christ interests us, we will avoid them in order to become peaceful enough to receive him.

3. We can choose to dwell in thought and word on those things which create peace inside us. Here there is room for all our creativity. We need only look carefully and ask, "Has this thought or action brought me peace inside?" Soon, we will easily know what makes for our peace. Let's cherish and repeat these thoughts and actions, to foster an untroubled center within us where Christ may dwell.

A second quality which the Last Discourse emphasizes is loving Jesus Christ and accepting his love and his Father's love. We can lay aside the modern, sentimental, emotional notion of love. It does not apply. The guide to love is given in 14:21: the one who loves is the one who obeys. If we want to know how we love Jesus, we check to see how we obey him. There is a certain rigor here, deeper than the "warm pink cloud" notion of love.

This obedience is not intended to be a result of warm emotion. This obedience is made of clear-eyed choice. We see that Jesus is good; we see that obedience is necessary; and so we choose to obey. If warm feelings help us, it may seem easier. But to obey the Master is the very core of loving him.

This love for Jesus is definite. It is demanding. If we find that our obedience lacks something, it will be fairly easy to find that "something." It may not be easy to correct. Nor is it necessary to correct it — unless we are seeking union with Christ. Only then is obedience necessary.

A third quality of union with Jesus is joy. In fact, the central verse of the Last Discourse is about joy (15:11). The reason for all Jesus' teaching is to bring complete joy to his followers so that his joy and our joy may be one. That is the heart of the union we seek.

How does one help joy happen? It is a by-product of other things, but we can do a little bit toward it. Here are two suggestions:

1. Accept what Jesus offers you in whatever form it comes. He offers, first of all, love; and that love has a stringent quality. What kind of parent loves a baby in such a way as to wish that baby to remain forever an infant? Because Jesus loves us, he creates circumstances which require us to grow into mature humans, capable of the depth of love which flows between him and his Father. Isn't that a stunning possibility? The first step is to say "yes" to his disciplined quality of love.

2. Check yourself to find the ways you block joy in yourself. The most common and most neglected obstacle to it is mental chatter. Our brains go nonstop, whether or not we notice. *Do* pay attention to that chatter for at least an hour. Notice its quality. Is it negative, full of resentment and fear? Is it distracting, pulling you away from concentration on the present moment? Just what does go on in your brain, habitually, when you aren't looking? The chances are it is keeping you from joy. You may be surprised, but welcome your insight. As you become more aware of that chatter, you can change its quality and redirect it in search of peace and love, to open yourself to joy. Then you will better hear Jesus' words of joy.

In these last instructions before his death, Jesus urges other qualities, too. Take time to read the three chapters and see what qualities you can find there. Choose one and begin to practice it. It could be your first big step toward actual union with Jesus Christ, because the daily practice of imitating him begins to make us ready for such glorious union. It *is* possible!

21. PASSION OF JESUS IN LUKE AND JOHN

Readings: John 18, 19
Luke 20:39—23:56

Do you know the story of Jesus' Passion well enough to tell it to someone else? The question recalls another: can you explain in simple sentences how to play baseball? Most of us, as Christians and Americans, would answer a quick "yes" to both questions. We might be too quick, however. Neither baseball nor the Passion story are as simple as we think!

Since this book is about the Bible and is not the Sunday sports section, we'll concentrate on the Passion of Jesus. We do have a clear notion of the main events: Jesus is condemned, officially escorted to a hill outside Jerusalem, and there executed by crucifixion. But, if we carefully do the above readings, we will quickly discover that there are two stories of the Passion. One is the report of the synoptic Gospels (Matthew, Mark, Luke), represented here by Luke's version. The other story is in John's Gospel.

That the stories are not identical does not mean that they oppose each other. It does mean that factual details and attitudes vary. When stories about the same events do differ in different Gospels, it is because of the various emphases and purposes of the writers. It is not necessary, not even possible, to know exactly what all the facts were. It is necessary to seek carefully for the meanings in the Gospels. If we hold differing stories closely together in our hearts, their variations unmistakably enrich our understanding. Sometimes, as in the Passion stories, the differences can also point to a special quality of experience for us.

In Luke's story, Jesus is the Paschal Victim: he suffers agonies in the garden; he is kissed by Judas; he is helped to carry the Cross by Simon of Cyrene; he refuses drugged vinegar; he is rudely discussed by his companions in death. On the Cross he cries out — once for forgiveness for his executioners and once to protest his feelings of forsakenness by God.

In John, however, Jesus is not a victim. Here, Jesus himself directs everything from his own position of power. In 18:4, "Jesus, aware of all that would happen to him, stepped forward" and began to conduct his own capture! There's no agony here, and Judas offers no kiss. Instead of a silent Jesus before Pilate and before the Jewish investigators, we see a Jesus who boldly talks back to them. In John 19:17, it says definitely that Jesus carried the Cross "by himself." Two others are executed, but nothing is said about them. Jesus on the Cross is concerned only about his Mother and his disciple, then accepts the offered wine. At the end he "delivers over" his spirit to God. The Greek suggests that this is not resignation but a very active deed.

In short, Luke describes the complete humility of Jesus, the amazing willingness of a perfect human being to be abased for love of God and other people. He follows the will of God through the suffering simply because it is the will of God. He accepts it as helplessly, suggests Luke, as you or I would have to do in similar circumstances (though our acceptance might be much less peaceful!).

John, though, reminds us most forcibly that Jesus was majestic, striding mightily through apparent humiliation — sure of himself and his Father, directing events according to the Father's purposes, always a person of dignity and power.

Both pictures are true to the nature of Jesus, who bore all the majesty of his divinity and all the abasement of his humanity. Both can be true of his followers too, in miniature. Calmly, we too can bear humiliations and suffering and helplessness if we choose to. All the while, within ourselves, we can remain careful that the real quality of the event is not destructive to our spirit. We can choose to accept — and to stand with dignity; we can go the way of pain — but keep our spirit close to God; we can accept the results of evil — but speak truth strongly in return, refusing to be defeated within. We can do what is required of us in the world, but strive to remain pure and courageous within ourselves, knowing that the world cannot rule our spirit unless we surrender to it. We can follow Jesus in suffering, trusting joyfully in his own majesty, knowing that our kingdom, like his, does not belong to this world.

22. PENTECOST

Readings: Acts 2:1-28

A friend recently said, "Catholics always gather around a mystery." He was referring to the Eucharist, but he could just as well have been talking about Pentecost. Even after all the analysis by historians, all the debate by theologians, and all the personal experiences of "pentecostals," the first Christian Pentecost is still mystery.

It is mystery because it is God's action. Many of the things of God are not subject to our reason. The precise meaning of the Holy Spirit and the speaking in tongues are two of them. There is no particular point in trying to analyze these things which reason alone can never decipher. But we can ponder a few aspects of this event so easily called "the birthday of the Church."

First, whatever exactly happened on that Pentecost, those who experienced it felt that God penetrated their very being. The signs of God's appearance were already familiar to those who knew the Old Testament: wind and fire. They often accompanied a divine appearance in the Hebrew experience. The Hebrew word for wind means "spirit" as well. When a natural event, like wind, is a symbol (as it is here), we can ask what qualities it suggests. Wind — powerful, invisible, coming from who-knows-where and headed who-knows-where — has direction; and it can stir up as well as cool and soothe. Wind is an appropriate symbol of God. His power is unmeasured. Though we do not see him directly, there is experience of him. That experience can be comforting, or it can shake us to our depths. But, always, the beginnings of an experience of God and the goals of God remain hidden from our minds.

In the Old Testament, fire, too, was a symbol of God: light, vitality, the life by which we live, power, and again a certain uncontrollability. Light makes vision possible, and God makes inner vision possible, giving insights and understandings. Fire warms and gives life, and yes, so does God. Fire burns according to its own nature and direction and is not very tamable by humans — like God.

So, the symbols of Pentecost made vivid an awareness of God's presence. There must also have been deep inner personal awareness; but this is not described for us, so speculation about it is little more than guesswork — not very valuable unless that experience is one we have shared.

Three definite movements are reported at Pentecost. The people are gathered in one place. They are together. (That reminds us of the original Hebrew festival of Pentecost — it was celebrated after the harvest was completely gathered into storage.) That gathering of people is the first movement.

The second movement depends only on God. He moves to empower his gathered people. He fills them with Spirit, with himself. They respond by doing new things, experiencing new understanding. They are filled with God. That filling, God's own act, is the second movement.

The third movement is that they begin to proclaim — that is the purpose of God's act in them. But they don't proclaim their own experience of Spirit, and even less their own ideas about what happened to them. They proclaim Jesus. They tell *his* story, declare *his* significance. In those moments of empowerment, they speak only of Jesus Christ.

Whoever called Pentecost the birthday of the Church may have been more fully correct than it seems historically. For these three movements have continued in the Church — indeed, in a definite way *are* the Church — ever since that first Pentecost. The people are gathered into one place. They are together for a single purpose. They hope to be filled, completely nourished, with God. Even when they are quite ready, the depth of their experience depends on God. It is his own mysterious act. Then the people go out to proclaim — not their own favorite ideas or experiences, but the story of Jesus. As Father John Shea has put it: the 2,000-year history of the Church which began on Pentecost is really quite simple. It is: "gather the folks, break the bread, tell the story."

The ancient event of Pentecost is celebrated every year. The Church, with its three special movements, gathers daily across the world — in every town. Will every day be a Pentecost for us? Are we open to being filled? And when we depart to our daily life, will it be Jesus' story that we proclaim?

23. PHILIP IN ACTS

Readings: Acts 8:26-40

There was really nothing else for Philip to do. But would we have been so quick? Philip was an evangelist and a person of deep sensitivity and inner power. So, when the angel spoke to him, he responded immediately: he probably gathered up a few things and set out to walk over thirty miles.

He headed for a particular stretch of road, "from Jerusalem to Gaza, the desert route" (8:26). Did he have a hint of what he was to find? Likely not. But with such an unusual beginning, he must surely have been alert.

So, we may imagine Philip marching steadily along, watching for whatever God wanted him to see. Then, in the distance, a carriage appeared. The Spirit told him to run and catch up with it. He did. The man in the carriage was reading aloud from the Book of Isaiah. He was an Ethiopian. A long way from home, he had been on pilgrimage to Jerusalem. Furthermore, he was an influential official in the Ethiopian royal court. Philip helped him understand what he was reading, with the result that the Ethiopian was immediately baptized into Jesus Christ.

Since the story is in Acts, we know that its purpose is to show how the Holy Spirit directed the spread of the Gospel to lands around Jerusalem. This is the main intention of this Book. In fact, some scholars have thought it should be renamed "The Acts of the Holy Spirit." When we look closely at Acts, we find very few apostles mentioned and only Peter and Paul described in any detail. But we do see the Spirit at work in everything to spread the Gospel. Philip is part of that broader movement.

But we need to apply the story to ourselves, too. It is unlikely —

not impossible! — that an angel will speak to us and send us on a trip without explanation. But we can learn from Philip's response: he simply went. The Bible is full of people like that. They live as close to God as they can. They try to listen to his will for them. Then, when guidance clearly comes, they move. They move immediately and without question to do the will of God.

How immediate is our response? Well, if the message came from an angel, we think we'd respond immediately too. Yet, we must ask if we are prepared to *receive* clear guidance. Do we live as close to God as we can? Do we *do* what we already know to do? Our lives bring us daily, even hourly, opportunities. The Church offers many suggestions about living closer to God. Do we study our faith? Are we available to help those who need it?

Most of us at times almost wish something extraordinary would happen to jar us loose from the rut of our "christian" decency. We feel that a shock might be good for our spiritual growth! And it might, but we would likely not be able to respond freely and immediately unless we were already prepared by long efforts to live close to God.

Philip, after all, had been through a lot: it was hard for a Jew of Greek culture to accept a crucified Lord. He had struggled to make sense of Jesus and his teaching; and undoubtedly he had to grapple hard with himself to become a person who *could* understand Jesus, who *could* respond to the Holy Spirit. The years before Philip could be used by the Spirit to convert the influential Ethiopian to Jesus Christ were perhaps all preparation — hard preparation — for this one dramatic task. When it came, though, Philip was ready.

Are we the kind of people who can be used by God? We have the opportunity to be. If we want to, we can begin this very day. Right in front of us waits a single, small, clear effort. If we are honest, we know what it is. It may be something to do or some-thing to practice being. We can make that effort right now. If we do it, we are one step closer to God — and our preparation for hearing God's guidance has begun.

24. PAUL I:
WHO IS JESUS CHRIST?

Readings: Galatians 2:20; Philippians 3:7-9
1 Corinthians 1:30
Colossians 1:15-18; Romans 8:38-39

Did you ever, as a child, wish that you had been there when Jesus blessed the little ones? Or have you wished that you might have seen just one miracle or heard just one parable from Jesus' own lips? A part of every Christian always wishes for a nearer experience of Jesus Christ, and we sometimes feel that if only we had been there it would have been so much easier.

At such times, another look at the Letters of Paul can help a lot. While Paul had an extraordinary conversion experience, still he did not know the earthly Jesus. All his experience of Christ came after the early Church was already alive. Yet, Paul's experience of Jesus Christ was his central experience, and it determined everything else in his life.

In Philippians 3:7-9 he tells us about this. He reminds us that before Christ he had devoted his whole life to the Jewish law, that he was even "above reproach." But now, he says, he has looked again at everything he used to value. All that was important to him before Christ he now considers "rubbish." (The original Greek word actually means "dung"!) He says that the only wealth he may have is Christ Jesus, and the only justice he may have within him is Christ Jesus.

That is a considerable statement for a former Pharisee to make! The Pharisees, and Paul was one of the most fervent, were convinced that wealth was a sign of God's favor. They believed that meticulous observance of the law was the only sort of justice God paid any attention to. When Paul says that now all those things mean nothing to him, he is saying that his whole life has been remodeled. So complete is it that Paul can write, in Galatians 2:20, "the life I live now is not my own; Christ is living in me." Christ has become, quite literally, all of Paul's personal experience.

It might be easy for us, who are much more lukewarm about Christ, to say that Paul feels this way because of his Damascus experience. But we ourselves know that any one-time experience, no matter how deep at the moment, fades over the years. Paul's experience of Christ continued, even grew. It was not merely the drama of its beginning that supported it.

We have a different head start toward a continuing experience of Christ: we have been brought up knowing of Jesus. We don't have to wait for special experiences. Every day we can make Christ as central for our living as he was for Paul's. We can do it by making a decision and by inviting Christ to live in us. Jesus Christ is just as alert to us as he was to Paul. The question is, are we as alert to Christ as we can be? Do we use the chances we have?

To help ourselves become more attentive to Jesus Christ, we can think about Colossians 1:15-18 and 1 Corinthians 1:30. Here Paul tried to express how central Christ is to everything, to the universe that we see and to the world of mystery that we do not see. There is no substitute for reading these verses yourself, but note this: in Christ everything was created and in him everything continues in being. In the Greek, that means everything "hangs together" in Christ. He is the center, and all depend on him. There is nothing without him in the universe, and there was nothing without him in Paul. Just so, there is nothing available to us without him, no matter how we may cling to our supposed "independence."

If we ponder this, it seems only sensible to let Christ determine everything for us as he did for Paul. We can begin by evaluating all we have and do, measuring it by Christ. We may hesitate because we already have a glimmering sense that, when we do that, something in us will have to change.

Yes, it will. Change seems scary, unless we are already hurting a lot. Again, Paul can help us. No matter how frightening any change becomes, he says, "I am certain that neither death nor life, ... the present nor the future, ... nor any other creature, will be able to separate us from the love of God that comes to us in Christ Jesus, our Lord" (Romans 8:38-39). Indeed, when Christ is central to us there is nothing to fear — and everything to hope for. Let us hold this close to our hearts until they open a little more confidently to that Divine Love.

25. PAUL II: DYING AND RISING/TRANSFORMATION

Readings: 1 Corinthians 1:22-24, 2:1,2
Romans 6:6, 12:1,2; Ephesians 4:22—5:2

If you are like most people, sometimes in a secret corner of yourself you have wanted somehow to *be* more than you are — bigger or better or more real. It's not an easy feeling to explain. Such desires are often within us, if only as vague discontent. Too often we may squelch them before we are fully aware of them as such, and so we may not recognize their significance.

Paul must have felt such a wish when he was very young. He did not evade it. In his early life he threw himself into living the law, to make himself "just," a whole person before God according to the Jewish way. Later, when he knew Jesus Christ, he came to see a different way; but he strove onward toward that inner completion.

For a thinking Jew like Paul, the execution of Jesus for blasphemy would have made faith in Jesus impossible. But the crucifixion was a central fact for early Christians, and Paul had to face it. It would be wonderful if we knew exactly what steps Paul had to climb within himself to arrive at understanding, but we only know the final outcome: " ... we preach Christ crucified ... " (1 Corinthians 1:22-24).

Paul's personal response to the fact of Jesus' crucifixion fulfilled his wish to *be* more. It transformed him. Saul the perfectionist Pharisee became Paul the Apostle. How?

Paul answers in Romans 6:5,6 that to die, to be crucified with Christ, is the first step. It is the basis for transformation. Essential freedom to be more than we are begins with the Cross.

Indeed that is a stumbling block, and not only for the Jews of Paul's time! Just as surely for us, it is a large obstacle. Who wants to die? Or, what does it mean while we are still on this earth?

First, we ask what it means. Later, when we get a glimpse of its meaning, we wonder if it's possible! It means thorough change, from the innermost part of ourselves outward. It means the center of our whole being shifts from ourselves to Christ. That includes our values and choices, the way we spend our time, responses to other people, even the image we have of ourselves. Christ becomes the reference point for everything we are, everything we feel and think, all we do and all we have.

But thinking of all that brings anxiety or outright fear. There is a reason. Change so deep, so pervasive, is always painful. Any one of us who has undertaken even to begin to change from our usual self-center to the Christ-center knows that crucifixion is not too heavy a word. It hurts. It feels like dying.

But it's all right to hurt because, as we die, Christ begins to live in us. (He *cannot* before we die — there's no room for anyone but me, me, me!) That is the whole point. As Christ lives in us, we are transformed. He increasingly in us and we increasingly like him.

Then Ephesians 4:22—5:2 begins to sound like a description instead of a command. Lying does end, and we speak the truth. If we get mad, it's quickly gone. We don't steal in any way at all — even thoughts or ideas! — and from our mouths comes only kindness. Bitterness vanishes. We follow the way of love, as Christ loved us — enough to die so we also could die and be transformed.

Paul's experience must have been like that. He became dead to all that had been important before Christ. For the ancient laws and customs, for self-righteousness he cared no more. They had been everything; now they were nothing. What pain and bewilderment must have gone along with that change! But we see Paul only after victory, when Christ has transformed him.

Let us remember, though, that Christ never forced Paul — and won't force us. Paul first had to be willing to allow it and, later, willing to struggle and suffer for it. His response to Christ *could have* been, "Thanks, but no thanks. Nothing is worth giving up me."

Our response is still open. Do we wish to be more than we are? Are we willing to start letting Christ re-create his death in us, by struggling against all that is not Christ in us? If so, let's begin now. Let's choose one thing in ourselves that is not of Christ and let it die — even help it die. With that, an opening is made for Christ's transformation of that "piece" of ourselves into himself. Cru-cifixion in pain always results in the transformation of resurrection — even for us, in Christ.

26. PAUL III: EUCHARIST

Readings: 1 Corinthians 10:14-17, 11:17-32
Complementary Gospel Readings: Matthew 26:26-30
Mark 14:22-26
Luke 22:14-27

What would have happened if the Christians in Corinth had not been behaving badly? Is there a chance that Paul might never have written about the institution of the Eucharist — and we might not have had his record of it? Well, probably, it still would have come down to us, for God works in many wonderful ways. Paul did write about it, though, because the Corinthian Christians were carousing at their sacrificial meal!

It seems probable that Paul wrote this Letter to the Corinthians about twenty years after Jesus' Resurrection. It is the earliest account we have of the Lord's Last Supper with his disciples. (The Gospel stories all came later. You may want to read them, too, as listed above.) So, we actually know very little about the early communities' celebration of their ritual meal in memory of Jesus Christ.

What we do have is reliable. Paul gives it in 1 Corinthians 11:23-26. Paul notes that he has this information directly "from the Lord" (verse 23), which means that he received it in a revelation from the risen Christ. Because of that, Paul kept it sacred and passed it along carefully to his newly initiated Christians. So it has come through the years to us.

As with many things in the Bible, we have the essentials; but they don't answer all our questions. Wouldn't it be wonderful if we could sit down with Paul and ask him just what the Eucharistic celebration meant to him and to his communities? As it is, we do have a hint or two.

One hint is 1 Corinthians 10:16-17, where Paul says the cup and the bread are a sharing in the blood and the body of Christ and that the oneness of the loaf makes us all one.

That implies that we Christians are enormously privileged: we can share concretely in Jesus Christ himself, that is, we can be "a part" of who he is, for we participate in his very body.

Further, that body is *one* body. We humans rarely think of ourselves as deeply connected to any self but the self inside "my own skin." Paul is saying that Christians who celebrate the Eucharist are all one body, as if we somehow all occupied a single skin! We have the privilege, because of Christ, to share in each other's lives not merely abstractly but really. What each of us does affects the others. What each of us *is* affects the others. This limits our room to "do as we please." It limits our selfishness. We need that help.

So sacred is the Eucharist that if we participate unworthily, or without "recognizing the body" there (11:27,29), we *create* disunity, discord, and bondage for ourselves. Paul says we also make ourselves sick (11:30). We are asked, then, to examine ourselves (11:28) so those things don't happen.

Recognizing the body, for Paul, is more than mental agreement that Jesus Christ is really present in the Eucharist. It is a soul-deep acknowledgment that because I receive Christ I am joyfully and lovingly bound to all my fellow receivers. Do we think of that at Communion?

The implications are staggering. Not only is our ritual sign of peace a *necessary* expression of our oneness, but we lie to ourselves and to God if we give it without meaning it. Or if we refuse that sign to our neighbor and then receive Communion, we also lie. Of course, it goes further. The oneness extends to forgiveness, to being genuinely a seeker of harmony with all our brothers and sisters, even at considerable cost to ourselves. After all, it cost Jesus — death!

Such unity can be real and concrete. In fact, it must be. It may take a lifetime for us to let it come fully alive in us, but each time we celebrate the Eucharist we can take another step toward oneness. We can ponder anew Paul's words: "Every time, then, you eat this bread and drink this cup, you proclaim the death of the Lord ... " (11:26). We share in the body of Christ because we proclaim his death. We really achieve a sharing in that body with each other, insofar as we die to our selfishness in order to acknowledge the whole body in the Eucharistic celebration and daily in our lives.

27. HEBREWS

Readings: Hebrews 1—13
    or 5:1-4, 7-10, 4:14-16, 7:27, 8:3, 13:15-17

One of the richest Books in the New Testament is Hebrews. It is also one of the most often neglected, perhaps because it is a difficult and complex Book. Yet, it has greatly influenced Christian understanding of Jesus Christ, both in his earthly experience and in his present glory. Further, it will expand the liturgy's meaning for us and offer insight beyond the physical ritual. Even a once-over reading will clarify much of the Mass.

Hebrews (contrary to what we often hear) was probably not written by Paul. It is not like the thought in Paul's Letters. It also reflects a later time, that is, as much as thirty years after Paul's death. It does seem to have been written for Christians in need of encouragement and instruction. It is not exactly a letter but, rather, like an essay which shows a lot of thought about the relation of Jesus to the development of Jewish religious thinking that had preceded him.

Whatever its origins, it is very worthwhile reading. Here we have space only to try to understand a couple of ideas from Hebrews, but you are urged to read, even study, Hebrews for yourself.

According to Hebrews 5:1-4, the purpose of the priest is "to offer gifts and sacrifices for sins. . . . for himself as well as for the people." This is an honor and no man chooses it for himself. It is granted by God.

What is a sacrifice? When we sacrifice, we take something of our own, or something that represents a part of ourselves, and set it aside. It is then separated (the original meaning of "holy").

We consecrate it uniquely to God. Then we receive back a part of our gift, now sacred; and in the receiving we ourselves are drawn more toward holiness. When this is done ritually, as in the liturgy, the priest is the active one; he represents us to God in the giving and represents God to us in our receiving.

Jesus is the high priest who has performed this priestly sacrifice in its perfect form. Hebrews tells us that Jesus "offered prayers and supplications with loud cries and tears to God . . . and he was heard . . . " (5:7). So, Jesus, while on earth, cried out to the Father for salvation from death, not only for himself but for us. God heard him. Death became not the end but a passage. In 4:14-16, Hebrews says we now "have a great high priest who has passed through the heavens . . . " and who can "sympathize with our weakness." So, Jesus is the perfect one to represent us to the Father and to represent the Father to us. He is the perfect one to make sacrifice.

In 8:3 it is pointed out that Jesus, too, must offer something. We already know what that "something" was, don't we? Jesus, as priest for us, offered himself as the sacrifice (7:27). He didn't offer just a part of himself or something that represented himself: he offered all of himself — *to* God *for* us.

It is often said that Christians are "priestly people." That means, for one thing, that we too may offer sacrifice. In Hebrews 13:15-17 we learn what our sacrifice may be: praise, good deeds, generosity, and obedience to our leaders in Christ. It even says, "God is pleased by sacrifices of that kind." Of course these are good things, but how are they sacrifices?

They are sacrifices because in each one of them we offer a bit of ourselves to God for consecration. In the offering, some little part of our ego-self has to be let go. In praise, for example, we abandon credit for the thing we appreciate. We give that "credit" to God in gratitude. In good deeds we must often give away our time and energy to benefit someone else, instead of furthering our own interests. Generosity is a readiness to give up something we want or have, so we offer to God a little of our attachment to things or to circumstances. Obedience clearly means that we offer a part of our very will to God through the will of the leader. It may be especially hard to let go of our ego in this way because it is so easy to think we know the better way.

If we offer these sacrifices to Jesus Christ, our high priest, he will sanctify them and return a portion of their new holiness to us. We receive joy in praising; a holy freedom enters our hearts in good deeds and generous giving; peace is the fruit of obedience. No sacrifice is without its sanctifying quality — and ours, made through Jesus Christ, becomes part of his, to take away the sin from our lives. Then there is left a joyful and loving life, which is exactly the point of the whole thing. It is for that quality of life that Jesus made his own ultimate sacrifice.

28. REVELATION

Readings: Revelation 2:2-4, 3:1-3,15-21, 12:7-12, 19:1-10, 22:1-5

Times were hard for Christians at the end of the first century. The Roman Empire was not in good shape economically or politically. In some places upheaval threatened. Elsewhere it was in full swing! Jerusalem's temple had been destroyed in the year 70, and soon after that came the final painful separation between Jews and Christians. No longer could a person worship in the synagogue and be a follower of Jesus Christ. Christians were viewed by the Romans with increasing suspicion and were sometimes oppressed and persecuted. No one could guess the future, but there was a great desire for Jesus' return to save his Christian people from such confusing and frightening circumstances. They longed for the reign of God *on earth.*

In the midst of their dilemmas, a vision was given to one, John by name. We don't know who he was, but scholars do not think he was John of the Twelve Apostles. Whoever he was, he recorded the vision with his reflections, and we have it as the Book of Revelation. It is appropriately the last Book in the New Testament, since it pictures vividly the struggles of the Church in the world and the final victory of Jesus Christ and of his faithful.

Revelation is written as a Christian apocalypse. (See chapter 15 where apocalyptic writing is described.) It is a highly symbolic Book. The key to the ancient symbols is largely lost, though we can decode some of them. We should not insist that every detail stand for something. More important, we should not try to apply the symbols to twentieth-century events or persons or groups. If we avoid these two things (which are faulty interpretations), we can find a great message of hope and glory in Revelation. To put its message more simply and much less interestingly than the Book itself, it is this: Be faithful! Be prepared! Be full of hope! The Lord is in control of everything. Therefore rejoice in advance!

You are familiar with some figures from Revelation — the four horsemen, the scarlet harlot, the seven seals, the woman about to bear her child. Recall those (or better, reread them), then look at 12:10,11. Here is pure elation: "Now have salvation and power come! Now is the reign of our God and his Anointed One! The accuser of our brothers is cast out and defeated! So rejoice!" (paraphrased) This is the end of the "war in heaven." God's servants, majestic and compassionate, are the victors.

The battle shifts, then, to earth, and plagues and terrors follow. But victory is sure, and it comes. There is general rejoicing:

Salvation, glory and might belong to our God. . . .
He has condemned the great harlot
 who corrupted the earth. . . .
 Alleluia!
The Lord is king. . . .
Let us rejoice and be glad,
 and give him glory! (19:1,2,6,7)

There are no guarantees here for individual welfare on earth, for there is much suffering. That raises a question we, today, have special trouble with. But at the base of that question is the less polite one: "What will happen to me?" That is not so much the concern of the convinced Christian. The Christian concern is the victory of Jesus Christ. And the guarantee in Revelation is that the Lord is in control, and those who are faithful will be given their spiritual place with him. They need not worry but only remain faithful to him.

What does it mean to be faithful? Here are three clues. (More can be found in the first three chapters.)

First, we can prepare ourselves by being fervent in loving (2:4). Other things are good too, but this is central because it is the most direct route to the heart of God who is love.

Second, we can rouse ourselves out of the sleepy complacency that gives mental assent to Christian truths. Assent is not enough. We can prepare ourselves for new life in God only by living that life here, now. Christianity is practical living and must find concrete expression in us or it is worthless. Let us not think too easily that calling him "Lord" will assure us of anything! (See 3:1-3.)

Third, instead of being lukewarm about our faith, we can put out some effort to enliven our Christianity. We can make a statement with our lives that is so strong we will be noticed! The perhaps too familiar question is worth considering: if Christians were tried as criminals, would you be convicted?

If we are faithful and prepared, then hope is fully ours because God rules. We can look forward to a new world, where we "will need no light from lamps or the sun, for the Lord God shall give them light, and they shall reign forever" (22:5).

May that light be our aim!

Conclusion

Readings: 2 Timothy 3:15-17; 2 Peter 1:20,21
John 5:39

It may seem a bit late for these readings, after we have spent so many pages exploring the Scriptures. Yet, it is good to look back over what we have done and review the purpose of all this reading and writing.

Scripture speaks about itself in only a few places, except when the New Testament refers to the Old Testament to show that a particular word has been fulfilled in Jesus Christ. In a comment about such references, the Letter called 2 Peter reminds us that no prophecy is a "personal interpretation." That is, the prophecy in Scripture is not the result of someone sitting down and analyzing the situation and making a pronounce-ment. That would be like a TV news analyst! Scripture is not like that.

2 Peter goes on to say that in Scripture "men impelled by the Holy Spirit have spoken under God's influence." This is carefully and precisely put. We know little of the mechanics inside a person when he or she is inspired of God. The discussion about how inspiration works has gone on for centuries and isn't likely to end soon. But we are clear about one thing: Catholic Christians do not regard Scripture as word-for-word dictation by God to a human secretary. We do not believe it happens that way. Neither is any of Scripture merely a human invention. It is influ-enced by human situations, certainly, but it always comes from God primarily. 2 Peter says, simply, it is "impelled by the Spirit . . . under God's influence." No details are given.

That is enough to tell us, though, the essential thing: Scripture brings us a vital message that affects us directly because we are part of the universe and, particularly, because we are part of the household of faith in Jesus Christ.

The Letter called 2 Timothy (also not written by Paul, in spite of the usual title) gives us more to think about. It says Scripture is "the source of the wisdom which through faith in Jesus Christ leads to salvation." Scripture does not stand on its own. It leads to faith in Christ, which alone can bring us to salvation. In John 5:39 a similar comment is made. Jesus says,

Search the Scriptures

in which you think you have eternal life —

they also testify on my behalf.

That is, they point to Jesus; the Scripture is not the goal of everything. It is a beginning point. It invites us to a living experience. If Scripture does not answer all our questions, that may be the reason. God wants people to discover some realities for themselves, in their own inner lives. Some things can be understood only in the living of them. Scripture motivates us to give ourselves to Christ, and in the living of that gift we will discover all we need to understand.

Along the way we will sometimes need help. 2 Timothy tells us that Scripture is good "for teaching — for reproof, correction, and training in holiness..." (3:16). Scripture, then, is good instruction, good direction. We may think that Scripture should explain things — but it doesn't always! The theologians are better explainers. Scripture, when followed, is *training* in holiness. That means its contents must be put into practice, regularly and definitely. Scripture is a kind of coach who trains us in the way of true holiness.

When we view the Bible as 2 Timothy does — as a practical help for growth — it suddenly becomes almost too rich, too challenging. There is so much there to practice, to explore. Some of those most impractical sounding ideas, when tried, actually prove to be the most helpful of all. But one only knows that if one tries them!

2 Timothy suggests that Scripture be used as a teacher for Christian life, a guide who won't let us get too far afield. This guide can tell us when we've got to change something ourselves, to correct our direction, and how to proceed toward holiness. Now that we've been reading so much about it, why not begin again and practice everything along the way?

Isn't that what it's really all about? Aren't we all called, invited, urged to become holy? It is no abstract invitation. It's an utterly concrete, daily invitation. God has given us that wonderful chance. Christ opened the door to us. He has given us the Scriptures to help us *do* — that is, to help us become actually holy. There is no higher possibility in human life. Let's go toward it together, Scripture in hand, prayer in heart.